Ridge Stories

Ridge Stories

❧

Herding Hens, Powdering Pigs, and Other Recollections from a Boyhood in the Driftless

Gary Jones

WISCONSIN HISTORICAL SOCIETY PRESS

Published by the Wisconsin Historical Society Press
Publishers since 1855

The Wisconsin Historical Society helps people connect to the past by collecting, pre-
serving, and sharing stories. Founded in 1846, the Society is one of the nation's finest
historical institutions.
Join the Wisconsin Historical Society: wisconsinhistory.org/membership

The front cover image showing Gary Jones as a boy on his family farm is courtesy of the
Jones family.

A number of the essays in this book appeared in a different form in earlier publications,
including the *Milwaukee Journal*, the *Milwaukee Sentinel*, *Cityside* (Milwaukee), and the
Ocooch Mountain News (Gillingham, WI). They have been edited and updated with new
material for this volume.

Printed in Wisconsin, USA
Cover design by Ryan Scheife, Mayfly Design
Typesetting by Wendy Holdman Design

23 22 21 20 19   1 2 3 4 5

Library of Congress Cataloging-in-Publication Data
Names: Jones, Gary, 1944– author.
Title: Ridge stories : herding hens, powdering pigs, and other recollections from a
    boyhood in the Driftless / Gary Jones.
Description: Madison : Wisconsin Historical Society Press, [2019]
Identifiers: LCCN 2019010818| ISBN 9780870209239 (pbk. : alk. paper) |
    ISBN 9780870209246 (e-book)
Subjects: LCSH: Jones, Gary, 1944—-Childhood and youth. | Richland County
    (Wis.)—Social life and customs. | Dairy farms—Wisconsin—Richland County. |
    Country life—Wisconsin—Richland County. | Richland County (Wis.)—
    Biography. | Driftless Area—Social life and customs. | Driftless Area—Biography.
Classification: LCC F587.R4 J66 2019 | DDC 977.5/75—dc23 LC record available at
    https://lccn.loc.gov/2019010818

To my wife, Lu, who not only encouraged me to write this book, but has heard the stories so many times that she knows them as well as I do, and to my granddaughter Julia, who inherits these stories and may pass them along to her children.

Contents

Introduction

"Does the wind always blow this way?" a traveling salesman once asked my father.

"No," Paw replied. "Sometimes it blows that-a-way."

Wind was a fact of life during my boyhood on our ridge farm. Fields of alfalfa and oats rippled in the wind like ocean waves, and during summer when the haymow was empty, the barn creaked like a schooner struggling in high seas. Elm trees frantically waved their limbs as if fearing they might be yanked out by their roots, and my mother's laundry on the clothesline flapped like panic-stricken semaphores.

Sometimes when I crossed the road between our house and barn, I considered putting rocks in my pockets as ballast.

The winter wind blew drifts of snow. Because country road banks bristled with brush, the hilltops filled with snow, subsequently blocking the passage of school buses and milk trucks. When I was in the eighth grade and read John Greenleaf Whittier's poem *Snow-Bound*, I felt that I could relate.

Our farm was located on a high spot on Pleasant Ridge offering panoramic views of ridge fields separated by forested valleys, and at night distant yard lights mingled with the twinkling stars overhead. And just as County Highway D divided our farm to the north and south, Si Breese Lane marked the western boundary between our eighty-acre homeplace in Willow Township and the one hundred in Rockbridge, both in Richland County, part of Wisconsin's Driftless Area.

But the wind we sometimes cursed enabled my great-grandfather Isaac Johnson to farm the land. Because the closest spring was at least a mile away in any direction, the only water that

I knew as a child was pumped from a well, once powered with a readily available source of energy: the wind. My great-grandfather had topped the white pines on our lawn to allow the windmill full force of the western gales.

His tall hip-roofed barn sat on a basement of stones that had been quarried from a bluff in the night pasture to the south. The barn featured a tin cupola—which we, like everyone else on the ridge, pronounced "KEW-puh-low." This 1917 building replaced the original barn, a log structure that had been moved from the foot of the cemetery and served as a church until the construction of the traditional white church that we saw from our kitchen window.

The classic T-shaped farmhouse, two-story living quarters and single-story kitchen, dated from the 1870s. When I was four, my family, in the spirit of modernism, tore the building down and moved into a remodeled cottage. Outbuildings included a large machine shed and small A-frame hog houses, all contemporaries of the red barn. The round, galvanized-steel government surplus granary, the corn cribs, and the white frame chicken house were added a generation later.

Buildings on Pleasant Ridge farms varied, but each homestead had a windmill.

In 1937, a few years before my birth, power lines brought electricity to the ridge, and our fan blades came down, although the tower remained. In the 1950s when television signals were beamed in the direction of the ridge, my father topped it with an antenna turned by a rotary device in the hope of coaxing snowy TV reception from stations in Green Bay, La Crosse, or Cedar Rapids.

But the advent of satellite dishes rendered the remnant of a windmill useless for any purpose. The tower came down, and eventually the barn, milk house, and silo, along with the outbuildings that had been rendered obsolete by progress and considered attractive nuisances by insurance companies, came down as well. Only the house—now inhabited by strangers—remained.

The utility and road maintenance crews have removed all traces of the scenic country drive that once passed our farm. The roadside hickory trees have been cut, as have the wild roses, sumac, hazelnuts, and lilacs. The banks along the road have been graded flat, removing wildflowers and wildlife habitat in the process. Snow drifts less on the road in this Driftless region, where wider roads more easily accommodate snowplows, and tree branches are no longer a menace to high-line wires.

As time passes, fewer remain who remember when today's farming corporations were only eighty-acre farmsteads with a dozen milk cows, or where the now razed one-room schools stood, or the saw mills, or the cheese factories. Many of the remaining farmhouses have become homes for those who commute to their work in towns or cottages for seasonal residents.

And traveling salesmen rarely make house calls.

When my parents retired from farming, I purchased half of the acreage as an investment both emotional and financial. Perhaps the adage is true that while you can take the boy off the farm, you can never take the farm out of the boy.

From the time I was a little boy in bib overalls at the Pleasant Ridge one-room school, I knew that I didn't want to be a farmer like my father, but a teacher like my mother. I enrolled in the school of education at Platteville's Wisconsin State College and Institute of Technology. In 1966, I became an English teacher at Weston High School, not far from Reedsburg, and married my college sweetheart.

My career was interrupted by a draft notice that sent me to the Army. After my service, I continued my education through the GI Bill, earning both a master's degree and doctorate in English.

After my retirement from Gibraltar Schools in Fish Creek on

the Door Peninsula, I worked as a part-time adjunct at what had become the University of Wisconsin–Platteville, teaching the class I had taken fifty years earlier as a freshman.

I hope to pass the land to my children and grandchildren, along with my recollections of an earlier time when Guernsey cows browsed in a pasture, Leghorn hens clucked contentedly in the henhouse, and Duroc hogs cooled themselves in a wallowing hole.

Sometimes I fantasize about becoming a farmer for my second career, but I envision an eighty-acre plot of land like my great-grandfather's, with twelve cows, a team of horses, a few pigs, and a flock of chickens—an enterprise as outdated as the Pleasant Ridge one-room school where I began my education.

Times continue to change life on the ridge, but at least the wind remains a constant, sometimes blowing this way, and sometimes, that.

If the Overalls Fit

Three identical men peered back at me, each clad in stiff, blue denim bib overalls. They put their hands in the oversized pockets and slowly turned from side to side. They were all smiling.

"It's not you," my wife said. "It is definitely not you." She was not smiling. "Go take them off."

I recalled that farmers used to rest their hands on their stomachs underneath their overall bibs. I tried it and studied the effect in the three-sided fitting room mirror. The three old men grinning back at me looked authentically folksy.

"Anyway," my wife continued, "the silly fad of wearing bib overalls in the city passed decades ago. You seldom see people in them now." She rested her hands on her hips. "Go take them off. Please. Why don't we go look at housewares instead?"

The overalls were remarkably comfortable. After wearing trim, low-riding, belted jeans, I felt a new sense of freedom in my overalls. True, the straps tugging at my shoulders would take some getting used to, but the looseness about my middle was wonderful.

I studied those three rural-looking chaps in the mirror again. For a genuine grassroots look, the overalls should be a couple of sizes larger.

My wife had begun tapping one foot. "Where would you wear that ugly outfit anyway?" she asked. "You can't teach in overalls. They'd be much too warm for gardening in the summer. And it's only fair to warn you: I won't be seen in public with anyone wearing foolish farmer pants."

She glanced at her watch. "Go take them off."

A couple of sizes larger, I mused. And I remembered old Gramp Jones. A diminutive man, he followed the custom of other slight and short farmers, habitually wearing bib overalls much too large for his frame. Perhaps it was an ego thing with him, seeing himself as the size of the pants he purchased rather than the little man who donned them.

One time, though, his oversized work attire may have saved his life, or at least, his male prowess. He was slopping hogs when suddenly one of the brood sows that had recently farrowed apparently felt that her litter was threatened. "Woof, huff, ruff!" she grunted, charging Gramp.

He unwisely dismissed her aggressiveness with a volley of curses, but the old sow, spurred on by porcine maternalism, was not bluffing. She charged with as much alacrity as a lumbering sow with two rows of swelling milk-filled udders could manage and sank her fierce yellow teeth into poor Gramp's crotch.

Luckily, the crotch of Gramp's overalls hung so low, no harm was done, other than to the fabric of his overalls.

～

"Here," said my wife, "try these on instead." She handed me a pair of low-riding, skinny-legged denim jeans. "If you must wear absurd denim pants, wear these. Go take those overalls off."

As I studied the three farmers in the mirror, I noted all the pockets the overalls boasted and remembered how farmers used those pockets. Take Victor Crary, our squirrel-hunting, pig-cutting next-door neighbor, for example.

In the bib pockets, Vic carried his pipe tobacco, a pencil stub, and a little notebook. In the front pants pockets, he stored his gold watch on its chain, his jackknife used for cutting everything from apples to pigs, wooden matches and toothpicks, and miscellaneous change, nuts, bolts, screws, and nails. The side pocket held a pair of pliers, a folded ruler, and his pipe. A bandanna handkerchief filled one back pocket and a worn leather wallet the other. I imagined Vic trying to find room for all his stuff in those fashionable denims.

If I wore bib overalls for teaching, I could dispense with my backpack. With all those pockets, I could carry everything I needed right on my person, and if, like Gramp, I wore them big, I might even have room for a paperback or two and maybe some carefully folded student papers.

Of course, I'd make room for a jackknife and a pocket watch.

"If you don't take off those overalls pretty soon," my wife scolded, "you're going to wear them out admiring yourself."

I unbuttoned the sides of the pants.

"Not here!" she gasped. "Go into the changing room!"

The three men now had gaping sides on their overalls, just like Banjo Schaeffer, the old farmer who lived out the lane to our north. A little guy like Gramp Jones, Banjo never fastened his side buttons and wore his overalls several sizes too large.

Perhaps he affected that unbuttoned look not as a fashion statement but for comfort, like one of those Southern houses with a central hallway, the front door at one end, the back door at the other. When both doors were open, a cooling breeze would blow through the hall.

But the seemingly practical choice came with risks. Ridge folks told the story that one day, as Banjo was walking down the driveway of his barn during milking, a cow that had been pastured on lush spring grass coughed just as nature made an urgent call. The open left side of Banjo's overalls made a perfect catch, the foul mess slithering down his bare leg and over his socks before spilling to rest atop his shoe.

It was unlikely I'd encounter any careless bovine behavior in my line of work, but I rebuttoned the sides of my overalls just the same. Shoving my hands into my pockets, I rocked back on my heels for a final inspection of the three rustics in the mirrors. Then I left for the fitting room.

"Finally," sighed my wife as she slumped against the rack of men's packaged underwear. A moment later she inadvertently knocked a package to the floor when I returned with the pants I had worn into the store folded over one arm.

I handed the clerk my charge card and the tags I had torn from my new overalls that I was proudly wearing. "To go," I said, pointing to them. "Please bag my old jeans."

As we left the store, my wife maintained a ten-pace distance between us and displayed an extraordinary interest in everything she passed. But I was undaunted. Shortly after, I purchased a second pair, this time for my two-year-old granddaughter, Julia.

Rubber Duckies

Many Europeans, I have often been told, feel that Americans are preoccupied with their bathing habits. That may be true today, but we were not compulsive in matters of bathing hygiene back on the ridge. We joked about the bachelor Hyde brothers (nicknamed the Skin brothers by local wags) who reportedly took their annual bath in the creek as soon as the weather warmed in spring, an ablution that had to last until the following spring.

But while we laughed and felt superior, the fact was that our own rubber duckies stayed dry from one week to the next. True, we took daily sponge baths, those spit-and-a-promise cleanups that involved washing face and hands, and sometimes armpits, with soap and water at the bathroom sink. But when I was small, a true bath was a big deal.

We had neither an indoor bathroom nor a water heater until I was eight.

Before that time, I remember having a hat-and-white-gloves visitor who requested use of the facilities. Always trying to be polite, I followed her outside and showed her the path to follow to our outhouse, a trail that led by Granny's former duck pen in the locust grove on the way to the chicken house. "If you don't see it," I told her, "you'll smell it."

The outdoor toilet, of course, was not for bathing, nor, for that matter, for washing your hands once you had done your duty. No convenient hand-sanitizer dispenser was attached to the wall. If you remembered, you washed your hands in soap and cold water after you returned to the house.

Before indoor plumbing became more than a distant dream for the future, Saturday night was reserved for bathing. We had a round galvanized washtub, like the ones people today use to chill beverages on ice for outdoor social gatherings. My mother put the tub on the linoleum-covered kitchen floor and poured a modest amount of cold tap water in it while a large teakettle of water heated to boiling on the kitchen stove. After adding the hot water, she finger-tested the temperature and, if necessary, cooled it with more tap water.

I was the first to be bathed in what was anything but a luxurious bath, only a puddle of water and the feel of galvanized tin ridges on my bare bottom. I suspect a rubber ducky would have grounded!

After finishing the milking, my father bathed next, in the same water but with a fresh teakettle of hot water added, and then at last, my mother, with yet more hot water and, for modesty's sake, the overhead kitchen light turned off.

On warm summer days, the galvanized washtub doubled as an above-ground pool for me. Early in the morning, my mother put the tub in a spot on the lawn that remained sunny throughout the day, filled it halfway with cold well water, and then let solar power do its work. By midafternoon, the water was a suitable temperature for my play, and with the unaccustomed luxury of several inches of water, I had sufficient depth to float a rubber ducky.

When an English major in college, I read George Bernard Shaw's play *Pygmalion*, a story now better known through the spin-off musical *My Fair Lady*. When the Cockney flower girl Eliza Doolittle commented on how much easier it was to keep clean in an upper-class bathroom than in her tenement room, I found myself nodding silently in agreement. We ridge folk lived close to the earth and to animals, and despite our best intentions, tended to keep both the residue and the scent with us, sometimes even when we emerged from the galvanized washtub, drying ourselves with an everyday bath towel, the ridges of the tub's floor still wetly engraved on our shivering bottoms.

Edna

"I leave the tin can for the hunters," she said, pointing to the one that was hanging on a nail driven into a tree. Many people on the ridge peeled the paper off a tin can, washed it with the supper dishes, and set it near the pump outside as a vessel for a drink of cold well water on a hot summer day. This cup would not shatter like glass.

Edna had taken me on a walk down the valley from her house. We followed the old packed-dirt logging road that had been cut along the side of the hill until we reached the spring that bubbled out of the ground at the base of Steeple Rock. We both drank from the spring, a novelty for me. As a five-year-old boy who lived on a ridge farm, the only water I saw was pumped from deep in the ground. The water tank in the milk house that cooled cans of fresh milk and the stock tank filled by its overflow were the closest things to ponds on our section of Pleasant Ridge, but I wasn't allowed to play in them.

Barefoot and dressed in bib overalls, I looked like a Norman Rockwell kid on a *Saturday Evening Post* cover. Edna, with her wispy brown hair and delicate frame draped in a soft house dress, reminds me now of the famous poet of the same name and era, one that I came to know as an English major in college.

Edna St. Vincent Millay appeared frail in photographs, with a mysterious vulnerability, even though her work revealed her as a woman who "burned her candle at both ends" and lamented "whose lips my lips have kissed I have forgot." My Edna, even when she smiled, seemed to carry that same burden of secret pain.

At the spring we gathered watercress that we put in a plastic bread wrapper for the journey back up the road and picked a nosegay of delicate mayflowers with their slender stems and pinkish pastel blooms. Through the trees directly up the steep bank behind the spring, Edna pointed out the stone spires of Steeple Rock, five sandstone outcroppings that were thought by locals to look like rustic church steeples. "When you are bigger," she told me, "we'll climb up there and explore them."

She took my hand as we walked up the woodland lane on the return to her house. The hike was tiring for a little boy, but we took breaks to spot chattering squirrels high in the trees and to think of appropriate names for the shapes of other stone outcroppings: turtle, hat, beach ball. After our wanderings, we returned to Edna's house.

When I read Edith Wharton's *Ethan Frome* in college, I pictured Edna's house, every bit as stark and hardscrabble as its fictional equivalent, no running water, peeling paint on the exterior, few softening touches inside. She put the bouquet we had picked in a water glass and set it on the table. Then she made a watercress sandwich and cut it in two, putting a half for each of us on plates, with a side of sugar cookies. She poured me a glass of milk and invited me to sit and eat.

Just as we were finishing, and Edna was telling me about a fawn she had seen on one of her walks in the woods, we heard my mother's footsteps on the porch and I knew my visit was over. Mother had walked me through the cornfield from our house to spend the afternoon with Edna, and now she would take my hand and walk me home, back to the land of the ordinary.

Edna's life was anything but ordinary, I learned when I grew older, around the same time I came to some harsh realizations about Santa, the Easter Bunny, and the Tooth Fairy. Her marriage was plagued by a number of problems, the farm by economic worries, and her health by serious concerns. The more famous Edna wrote a poem, "Childhood Is the Kingdom Where Nobody Dies." Such was my experience with my Edna, and now as an adult looking back, I recognize these grim realities.

When I was still a child, Edna became ill and was taken to the hospital, and I heard it whispered among the grownups that she had cancer. My mother donated blood because Edna needed transfusions and they shared a blood type. But Edna's health did not improve.

After Edna passed away, her husband sold the farm. At the auction my father bought a box of miscellaneous items to get a tool that he wanted, and we found in it a set of very old wooden-handled tin silverware. I asked if I could have it, and my parents said yes. That was more than sixty years ago, and I still keep it in a box of mementos.

Edna never had children of her own but seemed to share an empathy with mothers. In retrospect, I have realized that when she took me on walks into the woods, she was also providing my mother with a respite. Mother, I realized as I got older, loved her children but was nervous by nature. As a child I had thought it normal for mothers to cry when they were upset, when a child had been naughty, when a beef roast was ruined, when a husband was late returning from threshing.

She might have also noticed that I, a lonely child who found refuge in books, benefited from that time away from home too.

Edna hung a tin can on a tree for hunters who happened to be hiking through her woods, perhaps knowing intuitively that they might be thirsting for more than water, that sometimes, by chance, unlikely lonely people come together and form friendships.

Boyhood Games

As a child I was fascinated by anything "Indian." I made bows from springy willow branches and discarded binder twine. I rubbed two sticks together in the vain hope of producing fire. I marveled at the old arrowheads that my neighbor Barney turned up with his plow. And I amused myself running bareback through the woods, pretending to be a warrior.

Gramp Jones once told me that that the Grays, my maternal grandmother's people, had been Indians. As a child I was excited by the discovery that not all of my ancestors were pallid Europeans, all Bibled and buttoned up, but as I grew older, I realized that Gramp's characterization was meant to be pejorative rather than anthropological. The Grays were every bit as WASPy as the Joneses, and my grandfather simply did not care for them.

Sometimes, Gramp Jones would tell stories of Indians camping under the elms down on Rose's flats or cooking a rabbit—skinned but not gutted—in a boiling pot of water. Enthralled by the tales, I'd beg him for more details. He'd stumble through the mists of his boyhood memory, supplying no doubt as many illustrations from his imagination as from his experience.

When I was very young and went to Western movies with my parents, I was terrified each time the soundtrack pulsed with tom-toms and one by one horse-mounted Indians in eagle feathers appeared on a distant hill, scalping knives ready, peering down at the purportedly innocent white settlers in a wagon train. In school and in books, the Indians I learned about were less villainized but strangely generic—not accounting for the variety of cultures and experiences contained under the American Indian umbrella.

Not until I was in graduate school did I take a class in the history of Wisconsin and learn that the Fox, Sauk, Ho-Chunk, and Potawatomi tribes were the primary early inhabitants of Richland County. All Native-held lands, of course, had been ceded to the government long before my grandparents were born. In fact, as the national seizure of Native lands took place, Black Hawk and his followers had crossed my county in retreat, passing through the towns of Buena Vista, Bloom, Ithaca (where I went to high school), and Rockbridge (where my farmland is located). Twelve hundred Sauk and Fox warriors, women, old men, and children were reduced to a scant 150 survivors in four months.

As a boy who had yet to learn these realities, I wanted to believe in a romanticized ideal, somewhat akin to literature's notion of the noble savage, a trope I would later encounter in my studies. This image lent itself to some typical childhood pursuits—running free in the woods, playing in the mud, improvising weapons for play, and building forts. And while I could not claim any American Indian heritage, I wanted desperately to throw myself into that fantasy. The imagined connection helped to ease how displaced I felt on our farm, having taken no interest in the agrarian career Gramp had envisioned for his grandson.

I would cut a willow branch and string it with baler twine to make a bow that would loft sticks that I used as improvised arrows. My father told me that Indians shaped their arrowheads by heating flint rock in a campfire and then dropping cold water on the hot stone to chip off pieces (a myth commonly repeated at the time). I experimented without success using the wood furnace in our basement to heat rocks, but I remained undaunted in my pursuit of all things Indian.

Our heavy clay soil on Pleasant Ridge may not have been ideal for farming, but the pockets of pure clay that were exposed along the banks of eroded ditches were perfect for a boy who wanted to play at being a Native potter. I had read that tribes made clay pots without a wheel by rolling ropes of clay, coiling them into the rough shapes of pots, and then smoothing the inner and outer walls of the vessels. I dried my pots in the sun, and in lieu of a glaze, I used tempera paints to create designs.

Baler twine from the hay we fed our cows spilled from our barn windows during the winter. With visions of Indian blankets in mind, I fashioned a loom by nailing four boards into a rectangle and pounding rows of nails along the top and bottom pieces, inspired by the small metal potholder loom I had received as a birthday gift. I strung my loom with twine to make my warp and then proceeded to weave. Because I didn't use dyes, my textiles were the uniform golden yellow of hemp twine, but in my imagination, the design was colorfully intricate.

My father found talk of Indians less entertaining than I did, but he humored me as I chattered on about my interest while we milked the cows. And then one cold winter day as I returned from the milk house with a pail that I had just dumped, he asked me, "How would you like to make a teepee next summer?"

Unaware that a wigwam or longhouse would have been more appropriate to Wisconsin, I leapt at the chance to embark on such a project with my father. Nothing could be more wonderful!

Finally, another of Wisconsin's cold, uncertain springs ended. School was out, the crops in, and summer a reality. On a June morning, Paw announced that he had time to make the shelter.

With his ax in hand, my father climbed onto the little gray Ford-Ferguson tractor. I clung to the fender as we drove down to the valley and into the woods. Paw selected ironwood saplings that he lopped off with his ax and reduced to lodge poles. He tied them to the tractor and we dragged them over the moss and ferns in the woods, past the bull thistles and milkweeds in the pasture, back up onto the ridge and into the dooryard.

Next, we chose burlap bags from those stacked in the barn window casements. Outside we shook the gunnysacks to remove as much as possible of the dusty feed that clung to the coarse fabric.

On the front lawn, under the four old pines, we took the bags apart and spread them on the grass. Paw erected the tent poles and tied them at the top with twine. Then he borrowed string from my mother's hoarded supply in a kitchen drawer and made off with her largest embroidery needle.

Sitting tailor style in the shade, he stitched the pieces of burlap together to make the covering. His clumsy work-thickened fingers were more accustomed to the steering wheel of a tractor or the handle of a shovel than to the finer instrument of a needle, but as a nine-year-old child, I found his handiwork magical.

Finally, it was finished. Solemnly, the teepee stood between the four ancient pine trees. The tent had an awe-inspiring dignity to it, and in my imagination, hollow tom-toms were already pulsing in the background. Campfires sent wisps of smoke up to the heavens. No doubt a hunting party would soon be assembling before the door of my lodge, asking me to join them.

Ma came out to admire Paw's handicraft and agreed that it was indeed a wonderful teepee. I ran in and out through the door, showing her how well the tent flap worked. Ma and Paw then walked off arm in arm, each to waiting chores, leaving me to my tent and to my fantasies, where grain-infused burlap smelled remarkably like buckskin.

As an old man, I am still fascinated by American Indian culture, but after visiting reservations and casinos, reading history and novels, and watching documentaries and fact-based dramas, my feelings have grown more complicated than the simple enjoyment I felt playing in the woods as a boy. I feel guilt for the conduct of my ancestors, admiration for the ability of our indigenous peoples to endure, and humility for that which I still don't know about what it means to be "Indian."

Pleasant Ridge School

The photograph of the Pleasant Ridge one-room school's student body of 1952 included ten children and their teacher, Mr. Darold Fairbrother. The first person in the front row of the photograph, which appeared in an article clipped from the Richland Center *Republican Observer*, wore bib overalls, looking like an extra for a television episode of *Little House on the Prairie*. That was me as a second grader.

The earliest Pleasant Ridge School was built of logs in District 10 in 1858, located in the northern part of the district in Willow Township. Because no public transportation was provided, the community voted in 1879 on whether to move the school to the middle of the district, but the motion failed.

Mysteriously, the school burned to the ground the same evening the vote failed. Classes resumed in David Wildermuth's hop house, until the following year when a new frame school was built closer to the middle of the district at a cost of $750. That was the school that not only I attended, but my father and uncle before me. My mother even taught there for a while, one year having my uncle as her student.

My mother started me in first grade when I was five; kindergarten was not an option during those rural days. After I had been in school for a few weeks, Ma asked how my reading was going. "That's the problem," I told her. "The teacher puts a whole bunch of words on the blackboard, and I don't know any of them!"

She had a moment of panic, but as she had been a teacher, she remembered the look-say words that I needed to know and sat down to tutor me at my easel blackboard. Her panic turned out to be unfounded, as obviously I did learn to read, ultimately earning a PhD in English and becoming a teacher myself.

In 1952, the story of the Pleasant Ridge School was about to change. The next year, the Pleasant Ridge and Wheat Hollow school districts merged, with the original intention of alternating years between the two buildings in an attempt to keep the parents in both districts happy; no rural community wanted its school to close.

Subsequently, I attended third grade at Wheat Hollow and fourth at Pleasant Ridge. And then, because voters ultimately decided that the Wheat Hollow schoolhouse was the better building, the Pleasant Ridge School was closed in 1955, and I finished my elementary education at Wheat Hollow. The unused building was moved down the valley to become a living museum of one-room schools, the project of two elderly widowed sisters who reminded me of the Baldwin sisters on the television series *The Waltons*.

One-room grade schools were an efficient way to bring elementary education to sparsely populated rural areas. Teachers completed a one-year course of study at a county normal school and often taught not far from where they lived. Students generally lived a walking distance from their school. The student body was like a family of siblings in their relationships with one another, the older children both looking after and picking on the younger.

From an academic perspective, the school was nurturing and safe, but at the same time, it offered a curriculum limited both in scope and depth. For example, art instruction was a *Let's Draw* program on the radio. We all learned reading and writing and arithmetic, but for the most part we struggled to catch up and keep up when later we competed with classmates who had received an urban education.

While it may have lacked in academic rigor, our one-room school provided more than book-learning. Our forefathers may have seen a need to separate church and state, but on the ridge, the two institutions got along just fine. When Mrs. Myra Reagles taught at my one-room school, she was also the Sunday school teacher. It made sense, everyone thought, to recycle some of the same material in both the school and church programs, as Mrs. Reagles had her hands full with us. If Santa Claus came down the chimney at the Pleasant Ridge Evangelical United Brethren Church, or Jesus was born in the cloakroom at Pleasant Ridge School, no one minded. After all, people came to see cute kids say their pieces and sing songs, not to deal with philosophical treatises and theological doctrine.

Unless you had an accident that required stitches or were having a baby, a family took care of their own health and injury concerns. Subsequently, a part of the teacher's *in loco parentis* role included serving as school nurse.

If we injured ourselves on the playground, we not only had a Band-Aid applied, but first a swipe of Mercurochrome over the wound, a wonderful antiseptic that not only didn't sting, but sympathetically painted the skin a pretty orangish color. (No one worried about the poisonous traces of mercury the medication contained.)

The Friday afternoons when we lined up for the teacher to distribute goiter pills were especially engaging events. Some of us hated the big chalky tablets that contained iodine for prevention of goiters, but others liked their malt-chocolaty flavor and ate them like candy. Those who didn't care for goiter pills surreptitiously slipped them to those who did, and all of the tablets disappeared down gullets.

Playground supervision was a nonissue at one-room schools. As the entire school staff consisted of one teacher, who desperately needed a break, no one had recess duty. And unlike urban schools, no tall impenetrable fences marked our school boundaries.

Students easily slipped through farmers' line fences onto neighboring fields with our teacher's tacit approval. The instructor took advantage of the peace and quiet as she tried to keep up with schoolwork, trusting that the older kids would look out for the younger, and generally they did, much as bigger siblings did at home.

We sledded on the adjacent fields, played in the woods down in the valley, and built forts in the ravine. Luckily the belfry bell of the schoolhouse had the resonance of one in a church steeple and could be heard for a mile. At the sound of its tolling, we scurried back like Pavlovian puppies.

Today some of our teachers might have been brought before a disciplinary board and charged with criminal negligence for lack of student supervision. But no one pressed charges at the Pleasant Ridge School, as everyone knew the teacher had all she could do with that bunch of kids.

"I sure don't have the patience to deal with all those kids!" parents told one another. "I couldn't do it!" they agreed, shaking their heads.

Most of the time we returned from the wild safe and sound, rosy cheeked and out of breath, and to the teacher's relief, not quite as full of piss and vinegar as when we had scrambled out the door for recess.

One-room grade schools were already in a period of transition when I was a boy, consolidation well underway. Society was becoming more multicultural, more aware of the separation of church and state, more technology conscious, more concerned about special needs, more cognizant of safety and medical issues, and more litigious.

No longer were Gideon Bible folks allowed to distribute New Testaments to schoolchildren, nor teachers to dispense medication, nor kids to explore woods and creeks on their own during recess. Teachers gained colleagues and weren't expected to assume the roles of nurse, janitor, playground supervisor, groundskeeper, principal, social worker, and school psychologist.

One-room country grade schools were a colorful part of our past, and those of us who attended them cherish our memories. But like hornbooks and belfries, they had served their purpose, and yellow school buses transport today's rural children into the future.

Reading, Writing, and Sledding

Winters were different back on the ridge. The first snowfall was almost as welcome as the first day of summer vacation. On that day, all of us children loaded our sleds into the station wagon that picked us up from our farms and delivered us to the one-room Pleasant Ridge School. Except for Christmas break, most of the sleds would remain at school until the snow began to melt in the spring.

Oh, those wonderful rural recesses! We rushed out the door of the schoolhouse, galloped down the cement steps, and grabbed our sleds from where they leaned against the side of the building.

In no time we had scrambled over the woven wire fence that marked the official boundaries of the schoolyard and were zipping down the slopes of Otto Fry's pasture on our Flexible Flyers.

Mr. Fairbrother, our teacher, had been my mother's student when he was in first grade. An earnest young man with thick glasses and an unruly cowlick, he often joined us during the long recess that followed lunch. He enjoyed those snowy ridge hills as much as we did, often letting us enjoy a few extra minutes of recess. Under his supervision, we constructed sled jumps, ramps of packed snow halfway down a hill. Surprisingly, none of my classmates were ever injured flying on a sled over a jump.

When we weren't sledding, the fresh snow provided a canvas for other pastimes, such as a game of fox and geese. One of the older children led us in tracing the outlines of a huge wheel shape with center spokes that we called the "pie." The child who assumed the role of fox attempted to tag one of the other children, the geese. The tagged child then became the fox, as did anyone who in haste accidentally "cut the pie" by stepping outside the paths into the snow.

A partial thaw inspired the construction of snow forts. We divided ourselves into two armies that created snow walls out of huge balls of snow, perhaps two to three feet in diameter. Next, we filled in the open spaces with handfuls of soft snow.

Once both sides were prepared, the battle began. Mr. Fairbrother never objected to a snowball fight if all the participants were willingly involved. And schoolboy honor forbade the throwing of ice-balls.

A cold snap meant ice-skating. Because no ponds were to be found on the ridge, none of us owned ice skates. But we did rather well without them, pumping bucketfuls of water and dumping them down the path that led up the hill to the school. While the consequence of this undertaking meant that we had to walk on either side of the path as we trudged up to the school, it also meant that we could slide down the ice path as if we were wearing silver skates.

Everyone enjoyed the ice path. The big boys defied their mothers' strict injunctions by removing their boots and going down in their school shoes; leather soles fly much faster on ice than do rubber boots. The especially agile executed impressive turns as they flew down the trail.

Smaller children assumed squatting postures as they slid down the ice bed, ensuring a shorter falling distance and less chance of hurting themselves. The girls in particular delighted in duck trains. A group of children, each grasping the waist of the one before her, raced for the ice and then squatted in unison, coursing down the hill in a train formation.

When the bell atop the schoolhouse rang, we all—all ten of us or so—went slowly trooping inside to resume our studies. Before classes would begin, we had to struggle out of coats, scarves, stocking caps, and boots. Then we went to the front of the room to lay our sopping wet mittens atop the oil-burning space heater. When our clothing was wet as well, the teacher allowed us to slide our desks in a semicircle around the stove to dry in its warmth.

We were expected to work as hard as we played. As soon as we were in our desks, the room was quiet, with children penciling arithmetic solutions or geography answers into their Roy Rogers or Gene Autry tablets.

Through the windows decorated with paper snowflakes we had cut, I might see real snow falling to freshen the fields for our next recess. Then the silence was broken as Mr. Fairbrother announced, "First grade, stand . . . and pass," and clutching my Dick and Jane reader, I would take my place at the oak table in the front corner of the room.

But in the back of my mind, I was already anticipating the next recess and the return to our winter wonderland.

A Cold Lunch Program

No anonymous casseroles, turkey on a bun, or cook's choice awaited us in the one-room grade school back on Pleasant Ridge. We had a cold lunch program.

Every morning, I carried off to school the meal my mother had packed for me and stored it on the shelf in the cloakroom until noon. But even though some of us reached the point where we would rather have eaten a mystery casserole than another sandwich, I have good memories of the hundreds and hundreds of cold lunches I ate during those eight years.

I began first grade with a battered old black metal lunchbox (a dinner pail, to ridge folk) my mother had used during her teaching years before I was born. Since a school milk program had not yet been conceived, Ma filled a vacuum bottle with cold unpasteurized milk from our cows. As I had been warned repeatedly how easily the thermos would break, I carried my dinner pail as if it were full of eggs.

At times the sandwiches I consumed seemed like an endless procession of big bologna, but in reality, they were made of everything my mother could imagine to put between slices of bread as she attempted to create novel and palatable lunches. Cold hot dog sandwiches, for example, were a special treat. Some resourceful kids had their mothers heat wieners in the morning, tie strings around them for retrieval, and then pop them into their vacuum bottles so they would still be hot at lunchtime. And one family of children actually persuaded their mother to make them ketchup sandwiches.

Fruit, cookies, or cake and a candy bar rounded out the lunch. If another child had an item that looked more appealing, it became a trading commodity: "I'll give you my apple for your Hershey bar." And if someone forgot to bring lunch, the teacher expected us to contribute to a makeshift meal for that unfortunate scholar.

I was told the story of one mother before my time who routinely "forgot" to pack lunches for her children. When the situation became apparent, my grandmother started packing them lunches as well, discreetly slipped to them when they joined my father and uncle on their way to school. Other Depression era families made do, mothers packing sandwiches of homemade bread spread with lard. Hearing these tales, my own lunch seemed a banquet by comparison.

Usually, we kids were hungry by morning recess. To placate our appetites until lunch, we selected an item from our lunchboxes (often a cookie) for a snack. My father's generation had a similar tradition. He once told a story about his brother's first day at the Pleasant Ridge School. Pupils then also snacked during the morning recess. But my Uncle Vern, unaware of the custom, carried his dinner pail under a tree where, sitting by himself, he devoured the entire meal. At noon he cried, "My lunch is all gone!" and my irritated father had to share with his howling little brother.

Waiting for lunch meant a ritual of preparation. One older child's duty was to put a teakettle of water on the hot plate each morning at eleven thirty. At noon, cold water was added to the steaming hot water to cool it to lukewarm.

In the cloakroom, we lined up to wash our hands at an oilcloth-skirted washstand that had been improvised from orange crates. As the children held their hands over the dishpan, they each received a squirt of yellow soap from an oilcan and then a dipper of warm rinse water from the two students who had hand-wash duty. Once everyone had washed their hands, fetched their lunchboxes, and were seated at their desks, we were allowed to begin eating.

If the weather was nice, lunch became a picnic, and we raced outside to be first at the best spots. On cool but sunny days, the best location was along the south side of the schoolhouse. Otherwise, the teeter-totter was the most sought-out picnic spot. And sometimes friends would share a tree trunk as a backrest.

But whatever the setting, a cold lunch tasted best outside. Whether in the fall with warm leaves crackling a counterpoint to my waxed paper, or in spring with the sun warm overhead but the new grass damp and cool under my butt, the humblest peanut butter and jelly sandwich and the most ordinary apple became food fit for a prince.

Do Ghosts Eat Cake?

On the way home from the Halloween program at Pleasant Ridge School, I was euphorically rhapsodizing over my supporting role as a fourth-grade actor in a featured comic drama, *Do Ghosts Eat Cake?* In reality, the play was a scripted skit with an improvised set that included a sofa, creatively suggested by a blanket thrown over three chairs aligned in a row, and a small table that ordinarily held the school's radio.

The plot was simple. Three girls were having a Halloween party with cake as their refreshment. Our teacher, Mrs. Myra Reagles, had baked and frosted a small box-mix square cake for the play. Three boys cleverly hid themselves behind the sofa, and when the girls were not looking, snitched pieces of cake and wolfed them down to the amusement of the audience. The girls, puzzled by the disappearance of pieces of cake, suspected ghosts as the culprits.

After listening to me bask in nonstop self-praise, my father finally sighed and announced quietly, "I was in that play when I was in grade school."

It hadn't occurred to me in my self-congratulatory state, but of course my father had attended that same school as a boy. And no doubt every year since universal public education was a gleam in Horace Mann's eye, one-room grade school teachers had been recycling the same material for creating all-school programs.

Those spectacles were a mandatory part of the rural elementary curriculum, the teacher's only choice being whether the program would celebrate Halloween or Christmas. As a retired teacher myself, I can imagine the hurdle the production presented to an instructor who was also the administrator, janitor, playground and lunchroom supervisor—all while working not only single-handedly but without a telephone in the building. And I can understand the tension, too, as the school would be on display for a significant segment of the community. I can almost hear the teacher saying privately, "If I can just get this program behind me, I can make it through the year." (Some years the teacher delayed the responsibility, mounting a Christmas production instead.)

As a virtuous form of experiential learning, the school program had become a celebrated fixture in the curriculum. However, those of us who have spent lifetimes teaching know that the experience often makes a bigger impression on students than do any insights gained through that learning process. And the all-school program was a lengthy undertaking, at least a month devoted to preparation for the big event, putting aside more and more of the time usually allotted to reading, writing, and arithmetic as the production date approached. Students learned to work cooperatively, enjoyed the break from schoolwork, and involved their parents and community in the school, but perhaps at the cost of academic instruction.

Planning included a business component as well, with profits used to fund recreation equipment. Students sold raffle tickets for modest prizes, such as a bed lamp or a scatter rug. To theoretically circumvent Wisconsin's lottery laws of that time, we were instructed to give purchasers of a ticket a stick (not package!) of gum, so that they received something for their money other than a chance in a drawing.

In addition, mothers were expected to make candy for the event. Students would put the homemade confections in small paper bags and then hawk the candy before and after the program. Not surprisingly, the biggest customers of the raffle tickets and bags of candy were parents. In retrospect, I realize that the commercial ventures in a sense served as a sneaky referendum for additional school funding.

The rehearsals began early, learning the songs we would sing as a chorus, memorizing individual poems, and practicing the plays. I remember each year when we lined up in rows for the choral numbers, hoping I would find a place close to center of the back row, as we were always lined up by height. I recall the year I had been saving money in the hopes of buying engineer boots, footwear popular at the time and appealing to me not only because of the tough leather shafts but especially because of the height-enhancing stacked heels. I assured my teacher that with the purchase of my boots, I would be more than an inch taller and, in anticipation of those shoes, should be moved farther back and center.

The most exciting part of the production process was the transformation of our schoolroom into an auditorium. First, the desks were pushed back to clear a space for the stage. Years prior, some farmer-carpenter had made low wooden sawhorses to support two-by-twelve-foot planks. The boards made the floor of a temporary stage about a foot off the ground. The teeter-totter was detached from its mount, brought into the classroom, overturned, and placed beside the others to complete the stage floor.

A couple of fathers usually set up the stage and then strung wires on which to hang the front and side curtains; they were old sheets that a mother had dyed navy blue and then sewn plastic chicken leg rings to, allowing them to hang from the wires.

With the potential theater magic of the stage staring students in the face, none of us could concentrate on our schoolwork. That distraction was not much of a problem, though, as by this time, our studies had pretty much come to a halt, especially as we were putting the finishing touches on the production. We begged our moms for permission to bring throw rugs to school to put on the stage, to minimize irregularities in plank thickness, and a few small lamps for improvised footlights.

Our productions played to full houses, as parents, siblings, grandparents, relatives, friends, and even neighbors without children squeezed into student desks, took seats on random chairs and table edges, or leaned against walls. Of course, the audience of maybe thirty or forty people looked much larger because of the limited space.

As performers, we shone in the unconditional love that radiated from our spectators. We were too young to realize that our youth and potential, not our talent per se, earned the praise lavished on us. If someone forgot lines or sang off key, that shortcoming only endeared us to our elders all the more. The school was the center of the community, as many adults in the audience had sat in those same desks as children, and parents-to-be knew their children would someday as well, even if the furniture was moved to a different schoolhouse. And who knows, they might even perform the parts of cake-eating ghosts!

Farmers took turns serving as school board members, the elections only a formality, the office considered a part of the responsibility of raising one's children, of making certain that the circle would be unbroken.

The Pleasant Ridge School loomed large in my life as a boy, as our modest community's public institutions—the school, the church, and the town hall—fulfilled our neighborhood needs. As an adult, when I returned to any of those buildings, I was always amazed at how small they were, how few the desks, the pews, the folding chairs.

When later on I was cast in university productions, I learned not only stagecraft but my limitations as an actor. And that was okay by me. Because while I still enjoy the theater, all other plays seem to lack the magic of those I first experienced as a farm kid on Pleasant Ridge.

Ida

"One of these mornings," Gramp said, "Idie is going to wake up with a log up her butt!"

Ida and her husband lived in one of those classic Wisconsin farmhouses shaped like a T, with the kitchen attached to a two-story main section. An old log house had been incorporated into the downstairs, the interior of the logs concealed by plaster and the exterior siding, like a family secret. Nowadays, a trendy young couple might expose the logs for their rustic charm, but the people of Gramp's generation considered an old log building a sign of poverty, like carrying home-rendered lard sandwiches for your school lunch.

Gramp disapproved of Ida in general, as she was my grandmother's niece, not his. "Idie would drive any man crazy," he'd mutter. When her husband was plowing a field, Gramp said, Ida would walk along the furrow behind him, wringing her hands and worrying.

But I liked Ida and I loved her house, although the precarious state of the logs hidden within its bowels made me nervous. But in my memory, it is always a house of summer, comfortably settled onto an expansive green lawn under the shade of venerable white pines. The asphalt siding with its faux-brick pattern seemed clever and exotic to me, much superior to our little house with the peeling white paint on lap siding.

Inside, cool, smooth linoleum covered the wood floors, lacy curtains billowed in the breeze that breathed through the open windows, and painted dishes were displayed in a glass-fronted whatnot cabinet. All was silent as a museum except for the mellow ticking of a clock. Ida and Barney had children, but both were long grown and leading lives of their own, the middle-aged couple living a quiet existence on their small dairy farm. Ida loved children and always seemed eager to have my younger sister and me come for an afternoon visit when we were youngsters.

My mother would call Ida first to see if she would like some company, and Ida always said yes. "One hour," my mother would tell us. "You can stay for one hour only, and then you have to come home. You do not want to wear out your welcome!"

My little sister and I, her eight-year-old brother, walked down the hill holding hands, keeping to the left-hand side of the road as we had been taught. After our journey of a quarter mile, we would arrive at Ida's house, solemnly knock on the door, and listen for her voice.

"Come in, come in!" she'd greet us, laughing in delight, and give each of us a breath-squeezing hug. "I'm so glad you've come to see me!" Basking in the warmth of her welcome, I would feel like a lost child who had been found.

"We can only stay an hour," I'd remind her, speaking as the responsible older child.

And she'd laugh, and say, "I know, I know. Let's set the timer on the stove so we don't lose track of time and upset your mother!"

We'd follow her into the kitchen with its old-fashioned cookstove and pale-green wooden cabinets. She was a tall, gaunt woman with shoulder-length iron-gray hair and ruddy skin from her time spent gardening in the sun. She often wore soft, baggy slacks pulled up above her natural waist, a faded print blouse, and a grandma apron.

"Well," she'd say, rubbing her hands together after she had

finished setting the timer, "what would you like to do this afternoon? Would you like to look at Barney's arrowheads?"

We'd nod solemnly and follow her through the dining room and into the living room, past framed sepia-toned photos of Ida's children at various stages of their lives hanging from the floral-papered walls. A door at the far corner opened into Ida and Barney's bedroom, and if the door was ajar, I tried to inconspicuously peek into it, hoping to see a trace of one of the errant logs that threatened to injure Ida during the night. But at most, all I ever saw was a patch of flowered wallpaper, never a bulge of a timber waiting to burst through the plaster.

Barney's Indian arrowhead collection was housed in a cabinet with wide, shallow drawers, which must have been designed for storing maps. At the time, I assumed that furniture of this sort had been designed for collections of American Indian stone projectile points. We had seen the display several times but never tired of looking at it, always feeling awe in its presence.

The arrowheads, some of them spear tips, were sorted by size and arranged in artful patterns on velvet cloth in the drawers, as if the work of a museum curator. Judiciously, Ida would select two of them, letting my sister and me each hold one and examine it carefully. We fingered the flint as if it were eggshell china while she'd tell us again that collectors had offered Barney a fortune for his arrowhead collection, but he wouldn't sell it. Ever.

Barney had found all of the arrowheads while working in his fields. I used to wonder if Ida walked in the furrow behind the plow to pick up the ones he spotted and put them in her apron pocket to carry home for him. With the image Gramp had created in my mind, I pictured her wringing her hands over the responsibility of being in charge of something. At that young age, I didn't realize she might have bigger worries on her mind. After a few minutes, Ida would take the arrowheads from us, return each one to its exact location, and then, as if she were dealing with religious relics, reverently close the drawers. We stood silent, as if a prayer had been offered.

"Well," she'd say, "would anyone like to play croquet?"

We'd nod our heads and follow her through the dining room, across the kitchen, and out the back door onto the covered slippery-wood porch and into the back lawn where Barney had set up the croquet court in preparation for our visit. We never played croquet at home, and to me the game had an exotic quality, as if it might be the esoteric sport of rich city folks, like polo.

Neither my sister nor I was very good at the game, and Ida laughed good-naturedly when we made mistakes, erroneously sending balls awry. "I think you can have another turn," she'd whisper, fetching the ball and repositioning it for a second shot. Then she burst into spontaneous applause when we were successful.

Sometimes Barney would join us, but only to watch, quietly grinning in his loose bib overalls and striped engineer's hat, grizzled gray whiskers on his weathered clay face. Ida would announce that he needed a rest in the shade to escape the midday heat.

After my sister or I had managed to win the game and Ida had come in last, we'd have a lunch. The first stop was the kitchen for a huge oatmeal cookie carefully removed from a blue crockery jar. "Barney likes them big," Ida would announce, and he would nod and smile, chewing thoughtfully.

Then we would sit in a row on a daybed under a maple tree eating a piece of watermelon, spitting seeds onto the lawn where New Hampshire Red hens clucked happily as they waited to gobble them up.

"Do you have room for ice cream?" Ida would ask, and of course we always did. Ida kept her chest-style freezer on the roofed but open back porch, and she would make all four of us ice cream cones, piling high scoops of maple nut, mounds that would inevitably begin to drip before we had finished them.

A snack with Ida and Barney was almost a meal. My mother

would wonder why my sister and I weren't very hungry at supper time.

And then the timer would ding.

"Oh, oh," Ida would laugh. "We'll finish up the cones before you go."

But then Ida's phone would ring, two longs and two shorts: my nervous mother reminding us that it was time to come home.

After wiping our hands clean with a damp washcloth, Ida took us around the east side of the house to her rose bed to pick a tea rose for us to take to my mother. She'd find a Peace rose in full bloom, snip it with pruning shears, and hand it to me, the oldest, to carry home, reminding me to be careful of the thorns and to keep the cut stem up so the sap wouldn't run out and it would stay fresh for my mother.

Ida seemed to have a great affinity for all things verdant or natural, hunting morel mushrooms in the spring and ginseng roots during the summer. She taught me to identify ginseng leaves and amazed me with the price per pound she received selling the roots at Pulvermacher's Produce in town. And she transplanted wildflowers, trilliums, bloodroot, jack-in-the-pulpit, and mayapples from the woods to the shade of her lilac bushes.

But her tea roses were more carefully cultivated. They reminded me of ladies in flowered hats wearing white gloves as they sipped tea and nibbled crust-free cucumber sandwiches on a terrace. Ida's roses seemed to be a marker of a more genteel life than we lived up the hill on our farm, one that featured croquet and a small library of storybooks that had belonged to the couple's son.

As we walked up the hill toward home, I would intermittently bring the bloom of the rose to my face and press my nose into the cool soft petals, inhaling a scent as sweet and overwhelming as the Avon perfume my mother wore to her homemaker meetings. I bore it like a chalice, a reminder of the fleeting but valuable respite that Ida provided.

When I grew older, I saved my allowance money to buy plastic packages of bare-root tea roses and made my own rose garden beside the garage. Ida showed me how she took cuttings from a tea rose, removing the bloom, sticking the stem into a large clay flowerpot of dirt, and then putting a two-quart glass fruit jar over it to improvise a greenhouse. I experimented with one of my own roses and successfully rooted it.

When I was a senior in high school, I took photography as a 4-H project. Ida invited me to take a picture of her amaryllis that was in full bloom for Christmas. Barney, who had long suffered from mental illness, had ended his life by this time, and her house looked shabbier and older, as did she. Her son had come home to run the farm, and like his father, he was a man of few words, more cause for Ida to wring her hands.

She pulled the window shade to provide a backdrop for my photo of the amaryllis. With my Kodak Brownie Instamatic and its flashbulb attachment, I took a snapshot of the flower, knowing as I did that it would never win a prize at the county fair. It was difficult to make the lens see the flower as I was seeing it at that moment.

The plant stood before me like a somewhat awkward woman, the swanlike stem ending in the flushed face of a blossom, leaves folding like two hands nervously clasped together. The pulled window shade suggested something furtive, and I felt a vague sense of loss.

I smiled and thanked Ida for thinking of me and ate one of her oatmeal cookies, made big the way Barney had liked them, and remembered summer ice cream cones and watermelon slices, and hens picking seeds in her back lawn.

Putting Powder on a Pig

Our monthly 4-H meetings took place at the redbrick Buck Creek schoolhouse down in the valley. First known as the Fogo Valley Badgers (until someone pointed out that the Fogos no longer lived in that valley) and later renamed the swashbuckling Buck Creek Buccaneers, we dutifully stood to pledge our heads to clearer thinking, our hearts to greater loyalty, our hands to larger service, and our health to better living, for our club, our community, and our country.

And not only did we make this promise, we "pirates" on the banks of a shallow creek, but we offered tangible evidence by taking on 4-H projects, generally raising a pig or a heifer and then exhibiting the animal at the Richland County Fair. The county extension office supplied printed forms and a paper binder to keep them in, as we were expected to maintain meticulous records regarding each critter's growth, training, feeding, and expenses.

Parents volunteered to supervise the 4-Hers in their respective projects. After a brief general meeting consisting of the pledge and announcements, we subdivided into our respective project groups where the adult leader would ask, "Any questions?" And we would shake our heads: "Nope." Then we'd be free to run around and play until it was time to eat the lunch that our mothers had brought.

During the winter, we would enjoy 4-H-sponsored euchre

card parties as a fundraiser, student desks shoved to the sides of the one-room school and folding card tables and chairs the parents had brought set up for the event. Four people sat at each table, partners facing each other. The winning pair moved on for the next game, switching partners as they did. At the evening's end, small prizes were awarded to the top scorers, and of course everyone ate the lunch that the mothers had brought.

The highlight of 4-H summers was the softball competition with other 4-H teams. A father or two served as coaches, and we'd have a couple of Sunday afternoon practices before the series of evening games began. But the practices were not as much to pick up skills—we all played softball at our respective schools—as to assess the skill levels of the individual players for assigning positions.

In the abstract, playing softball appealed to me a great deal. In reality, my hand-eye coordination was severely compromised. I could not throw a ball fast and far, nor could I always catch one rapidly fired at me or as it fell from high up in the heavens. And throughout my entire history in the sport, I don't think I ever hit more than a single. During my grade school years, I saw limited playing time as a right fielder, a position that allowed me to be a part of the team but one in which I would bring the smallest liability. By the time I was in high school, I was fairly secure as a first baseman, again, one of those positions that required a lesser skill level. I remember the ongoing embarrassment as a high schooler coming up to bat for the first time and having the fielders move farther back, but then, after a demonstration of my limited batting skill, watching everyone move slightly forward on my next at bat.

Despite my limited strength as a ball player, our team did well. Not only did we have boys on the team who were naturals, but we had the Thompsons, a ball-playing family with one son and two daughters, all of whom were outstanding players. When the Thompson girls came up to bat, the fielders moved forward only the first time. And when the older girl was a relief pitcher for her brother, the older boys lost their cocky grins when she hurled the ball across the plate.

The county fair at the end of August was the culmination of the 4-H year. School had recently started, the softball games were at an end, and the record books were due. I remember sitting at the kitchen table with the blank pages of my record book, my irritated parents standing over me glowering, hands at their waists, helping me create "records" for my pig or my calf, my father pulling numbers out of the air for me and my mother scolding me for my irresponsibility.

But the county fair was worth the anguish. We were excused from school to take our animals to the grounds before the weekend of the fair, and I would stay with Gramp and Granny Jones, who had retired from farming and lived in Richland Center. Gramp would drive me to the fairgrounds, where I was expected to watch over my animal. But after giving my project food and water, I explored the exotic world of the county fair, trying my skills at those games of chance (even though I never managed to win one of the big teddy bears that farm boys gave their girl-friends), feeling intimidated by the carnies with their tattoos and eyes squinting through cigarette smoke, and getting up the courage to feign nonchalance as I climbed aboard rides that flung me upside down through the air. The huge outdoor toilet, filled with strangers, a lengthy rain-gutter urinal, and an attendant with a suspicious stare, was a far cry from the private privies at the Pleasant Ridge Evangelical United Brethren Church and one-room school.

For those of us 4-Hers who led relatively innocent lives throughout the year, the county fair provided us with our first exposure to the temptation of sin. We were farm kids, but we could affect a swagger as we walked down the midway, and while during the winter we might be content to hold a girl's hand, here we might brazenly put an arm around her shoulder. Leaving our animals untended in the exhibit barns, we assumed the demeanor of city kids, the boys masking our barn smell with Mennen After Shave and the girls wearing makeup and taking pains with their hair. To discourage fairgoers from going too far off the moral path, the Women's Christian Temperance Union dumped a shot glass of whiskey into a fishbowl every hour on the hour, bringing an unwitting goldfish belly-up—an impressive, if scientifically flawed, demonstration of the evils of alcohol.

~

One year I chose photography as my project. Earlier I had raised a Landrace hog, and while I enjoyed the drama of taking an animal to the fair, I knew that I did not want to be a farmer.

But a photographer! That was a horse of a different color. Rather than the drudgery of milking cows morning and night, in all kinds of weather, and slopping hogs that spent their spare time conspiring to escape their pasture, I pictured myself traveling on assignment to exotic places taking landscape photographs for *Look Magazine,* maybe even *National Geographic.* I would exchange my overalls for sunglasses and a black T-shirt and look artsy in the fine arts exhibition hall. For my birthday, I had received a Brownie Kodak Instamatic with a flash attachment; I thought I was well on the road to success as a photojournalist.

Most of the pictures required for the 4-H project were no problem—snapshot portraits of family members, landscapes, floral arrangements—and I thought I could easily point and shoot my way to victory. At the eleventh hour, I began shooting, but the one stumbling block was the picture story. The assignment: Take five photographs that imply a narrative. Recalling that writers are told to write what they know, I deduced that the same should hold true for photographers, and my mind turned to the pigs who had been my 24/7 project just a year before.

Landrace hogs were a relatively new breed at the time, slim, long-legged, and as white as the driven snow, theoretically. Through the county extension office, a local farmer had given me a gilt with the understanding that I would pass along one of her offspring to another 4-H member, like a chain letter. Now our hog lot was populated with Hilda's progeny.

My sister, Margaret Ann, was of an age that she was beginning to take pride in her appearance, fussing with her hair and begging permission to wear makeup. I knew she would like nothing better than to be a photographer's model, even if she was sharing the limelight with a hog. She readily consented.

My picture story would be entitled *Preparing a Pig for the County Fair*, and in my mind I quickly assembled the steps, thinking back to my own experience with Hilda. The first was training the pig for the show ring. In theory, the show pig was to be gently guided into the ring with soft taps of a wooden walking-style cane. The young 4-Her was to have practiced with his charge, accustoming her to the process, much as a dog is taught to heel on a leash. In reality, I made a last-minute purchase of the cane at the hardware store and entered the ring with Hilda, neither of us knowing what we were doing. Her eyes wide in alarm, she immediately pooped at the judge's approach and hesitated as she searched for an opening in the fence.

Margaret Ann emerged from the house, her hair teased and sprayed, her lips red, and her eyes blue-shadowed. I handed her the cane, and she walked to the hog lot as if she were carrying a scepter.

None of Hilda's daughters wanted anything to do with Margaret Ann. My one successful photo was of my sister and a pig on the horizon running at full tilt, Margaret Ann swinging the cane above her head as if she hoped to thrash it, and the trim, long-legged gilt comfortably loping along like a deer.

The second photo was meant to show the bathing of the pig. This time we confined one of Hilda's daughters in a pigpen. After checking and correcting her hair in a pocket mirror, Margaret Ann entered like a boxer's manager carrying a bucket of warm soapy water and a scrub brush. She had taken off her shoes, as she and the pig were both ankle-deep in mud, but we needed a pen if she was to have any hope of approaching within arm's length of her client. The photo looked as if this might have been a prelude to a greased pig wrestle, as my sister sloshed suds at her subject and swatted with a brush.

Because Landrace hogs are white, a champion hog should resemble fresh snow or a daisy's petals. As few possessed such natural beauty, the secret was to dust the show pig with talcum powder. While our pig air-dried and sulked in the pen, my sister resprayed her own hair, and I found an old sprinkling container of baby powder. This photo was more successful than the bathing scene, I thought, as the cloud of white dust that enveloped the sprinting pig obscured the blurriness of the picture and, even more important, the depth of the mud.

I needed five photographs for the series and was at a loss for number four. Hilda had not been a high-maintenance hog when it came to grooming for her debut. In a pinch, I decided a well-manicured hog would probably need to have the long hairs on her tail trimmed. But even with our wary subject confined to the muddy pigpen, this tonsorial exercise could only occur with a general anesthetic. For art's sake, I turned to a precursor of Photoshopping: in the machine shed I found a faded light gray length of rope that approximated the thickness of a pig's tail and frayed it at one end. I had Margaret Ann assume a sitting position holding a frayed end of the rope in one hand and a pair of sewing scissors in the other. The viewer was to assume that the remainder of the pig was off-camera, as I carefully framed the photo while my sister posed motionless, flashing a beauty queen smile.

The fifth photo was the finished product, a petulant pig in a starting block stance glaring at me from one corner of the muddy pen while I took the snapshot. Afterward, in the most colorful language that I then allowed myself, I told her what a bad pig she had been.

My picture story did not win first prize at the fair. In retrospect, I try to imagine the thoughts of the judges as they viewed my photographs. Did they feel a sense of outrage at what might be construed as a mockery of the contest? Or did they struggle to keep from laughing out loud at the efforts of a naïve country boy?

I never did get to travel the world as a photojournalist, but as a freelance writer, I've occasionally been called upon to provide photographs as well. I am more comfortable producing words than images, but still a point-and-shoot guy, I grudgingly consent. Fortunately, a digital camera helps to powder my pig, so to speak, and I'm a lot better about deadlines.

Free-Range Chickens

My mother was an early believer in free-range chickens, not because of a concern for their happiness or for a belief in organic food production. Rather, she was a pragmatist. If chickens spent their days in the wild, they foraged for bugs and whatever else they could eat rather than being fed a limited diet of expensive grain.

But letting the chickens forage for themselves was not without its downsides. Given the freedom to choose where they ranged, the front lawn was a favorite stomping ground, and the front porch, a lounge of choice. And they made their presence known by the evidence they left behind. As my mother raised white Leghorn chickens, the lawn would look as if two armies had fought using pillows as weapons of mass destruction. Equally evident were the myriad piles of white goo that clung to the soles of shoes, loose feathers sticking to the foul fowl paste.

Subsequently, my mother made use of the range house, which improved the appearance of our lawn but at the expense of the leisure of her eldest son, me.

The range house was a low building with a peaked board roof, its sides and floor made of chicken wire, the interior filled with roosts. The structure was supported on runners, creating a mobile home for the chickens, as it could be dragged by tractor from one location to another, leaving the accumulation of chicken manure that had fallen through the wire floor behind. During summer, it was pulled to a far hayfield, a distance too daunting for the chickens to walk to the front porch but a reasonable trip for a young boy staggering with two buckets of water.

Ma took her chickens seriously and had a rather detailed business plan for them, beginning in spring when she would buy chicks from Pulvermacher's in Richland Center. She would order one hundred sorted female chicks destined to become her next flock of laying hens, producing eggs that she sold by the thirty-dozen case to Pulvermacher's, and another fifty of unsorted chicks, the females joining the ranks of laying hens, and the roosters, who, after a carefree life on the range with admiring pullets everywhere, were destined to end their frisky short lives as fryers. The hens that had passed their prime as layers were ultimately sold as stewing chickens.

My mother placed ads in the *Richland Center Shopping News* in midsummer, advertising young fryers at one dollar each or a dollar and a quarter dressed. Soon after the paper was distributed, the phone began to ring with orders. I was given the responsibility of choosing who would live and who would die among the rooster population. Sometimes I'd run down my victim and grab him by his legs, but the easiest method was to wait until the sun was setting and the flock was crowding along the ridge of the range house.

The butchering of chickens was an unpleasant process for a child to observe. My father's task was to cut off the rooster's head with an ax. He had driven two nails in an upended section of log for the execution and would slip the bird's neck between them, stretching it before he brought down the ax blade. Then he would toss the victim to one side, and, as expected, it would run like a chicken with its head cut off. (My Granny Jones had her own equally grim method. Holding the wingtips and legs of the fowl in one hand, she stepped gently on its head, and then severed its neck with a butcher knife.) Once the rooster had fallen into repose, my mother would appear with a bucket of boiling hot water, plunge the bird into it for loosening the feathers, and then pluck the creature naked, feathers falling where they may until blown away by the wind, before taking the carcass into her kitchen to complete the process of dressing it, an ironic turn of phrase, as a dressed chicken was a naked bird.

Equally unsettling for a child was the smell of this undertaking, not only the unpleasant scent of wet feathers as the bird was plucked but also the odor of fresh, warm entrails being pulled from the body cavity and then the awful reek of pinfeathers being singed in a jar-lid flame of alcohol.

I wouldn't eat chicken when I was a kid. Not only did the butchering process disgust me, but I found live chickens off-putting as well. I liked the gentle, friendly bovine presence of our cattle, but chickens had nothing in their personalities to recommend their company. They were infinitely stupid beings, giving credence to the epithet *birdbrain*. I was a kind and familiar presence in the henhouse when I brought water or gathered eggs, yet they would squawk and fly wildly about when I walked in, much like teenagers at a Friday the 13th movie.

I couldn't take their treatment of me personally, though, after observing how incredibly cruel they were to one another. If one of the chickens sustained an injury that drew even one drop of blood, its feathered friends and neighbors would gather around and peck it to death.

And they had no sense of self-protection. Rather than safely bunking down for the night in the range house, the free-range chickens would crowd along the ridge of the roof, easy prey for the varmints that made the nearby woods their home. My final chicken chore of a summer day was to walk down to the range house as the sun was setting and grab protesting, squawking, wing-flapping chickens from the roof, toss them inside the range house, and lock the door.

One night, apparently, I didn't close the door to the range house securely, and in the morning when we went out to the barn to milk the cows, we could see a white trail of dead chickens leading from the range house down into the woods. When we followed it, we found that it ended at a fox den.

I'm reminded of a story that was told of a fox and a henhouse. It seems that a farmer had been having trouble with a fox killing his wife's chickens. When he heard frantic squawking during the night, he jumped out of bed, grabbed his shotgun, loaded it, and wearing nothing but his undershirt, stalked off to the henhouse, his farm dog at his heels.

Slowly and cautiously, he opened the door to the chicken house, peering along the barrel of his gun, when unexpectedly the dog pressed its cold nose against his bare butt. Reflexively, he pulled the trigger, killing most of his wife's flock.

In real life, protecting the chickens was slightly more dignified—but only slightly.

Once, when my aunt, uncle, and cousins were visiting us from the city, my mother reminded me, not for the first time, that I needed to carry water down to the chickens at the range house. "All right, all right!" I shouted. "I'll water those puking chickens!" I stomped off to the pump, filled two buckets, and trudged out into the field.

For some unfathomable reason, my aunt and uncle found my response funny, and for years after would quote me, "All right, all right, I'll water those puking chickens!" and then laugh uproariously. City folks, it seemed, had no understanding of the trials a country boy faced in helping his mother put a chicken on their table.

Charlotte

She came into my life the summer after my first year in college. No, this was not a summer romance, although she played a starring role in my boyhood fantasies. Charlotte was the sheep of my dreams, or more accurately, the product of my ruminations while mowing the lawn. Reality was another matter.

Ours was a country lawn that sprawled in all directions, and as the oldest boy in the family, I fell heir to its maintenance. Mowing was an all-day chore, especially as my mower was never state of the art. My father's small dairy farm on Pleasant Ridge was a subsistence operation, 180 acres (a good part of it woods and hills) and twenty milk cows along with a few pigs and my mother's laying hens. The machinery was vintage, some implements purchased secondhand, a few that were horse-drawn in an earlier life and passed down from my grandfather.

As lawnmowers were a low priority, we put up with a series of them, all disreputable. Paw would buy a cheap used mower, convinced that with his mechanical skills, he could recondition it to like new. With the temperament of a poet, not a mechanic, I rarely could start the mower and would call my father for help. After much scattering of his tools and sputtering of his curses, the engine would cough like an inmate at a TB sanitarium, and I'd be in business.

I walked along the section by the weeping willows, back and

forth on the main lawn under the four ancient white pines, over the sunken foundation of the old house, across the portion under the giant elm, through the rugged terrain we called Granny's duck pen in the locust grove, and then finally down the strip along the border of Chinese elms that Uncle Vern had planted as a windbreak. If the lawnmower was especially temperamental, the task would stretch into more than one day.

I knew the golf course–sized lawn was largely my own fault; I had taken home improvement as a 4-H project two years earlier. In my enthusiasm, I had tamed grounds that previously had been home to towering weeds and nodding grasses, as if I were a homesteader landscape gardener. I tore down a dilapidated garage and built benches with salvaged lumber. I constructed rock gardens and planted flowerbeds. Now I was paying the price, maintaining my country estate.

The noise of the engine and the Sisyphean task of trudging behind the mower gave me ample opportunity for reverie. And that was when I thought of Charlotte. Our neighbors down the road had had a flock of sheep when I was a little boy. The woolies were long gone, but the possibilities remained. They were excellent lawnmowers, I recalled, possessing unconditional fondness for anything green. If I had sheep, my lawn would be a smooth blanket of green, with the added Old English pastoral charm of grazing lambs. My balky lawnmower could sit in the machine shed sulking and rusting.

To my surprise, Paw agreed to the suggestion, and at the stockyard in town, I found myself high bidder on a sheep. I paid the two dollars and brought my new lawnmower home, confident that Charlotte would always start.

The namesake of Charlotte was a girl whom everyone knew at my college. The school of agriculture was populated by men except for one young woman, a capable girl who looked as if she could milk cows and plow fields, but sheep were her focus.

Unfortunately, behind her back she was a figure of fun for male chauvinists who, believing in a rigid separation of gender roles, referred to her as Charlotte the Sheep Woman. Now that women are well represented in agricultural science, I blush at our intolerance and lack of imagination. While I was excited to put Charlotte the Actual Sheep to work, my mother was wary of the project. Her father had raised sheep when she was a girl, and in the flock was a hostile buck. When she glanced at my dimwitted ewe, she saw the shadowy menace of a potential assailant and kept her distance.

I teased her about her phobia. Sheep have a reputation for vulnerability, timidity, and stupidity. Some sheep farmers even keep a llama in the flock as a watch guard. Reportedly, if a dog or some other predator wanders into the pasture, the llama bleats a warning to his intellectually challenged cousins, stamps a warning to the dog, and if the canine attacker does not heed the caution, proceeds to kick the crap out of him. I had read Thomas Hardy's novel *Far from the Madding Crowd* and been shocked by the opening scene in which an ill-behaved stock dog chases Gabriel Oak's entire flock over a cliff, all of the woolies plummeting to their deaths. Oh, if Gabriel Oak had only owned a llama, *Far from the Madding Crowd* might have ended happily ever after.

But as to the intelligence of sheep, one shepherd pointed out that a sheep might be lassoed once, but unlike cattle, never twice. They catch on quickly and duck their heads to avoid the rope. Their problem, it seems, is that like so many of our own species, they tend to follow the crowd, sometimes voting against their own interests. The only one who had anything to fear from Charlotte was likely Charlotte herself.

Shepherding a dull but stubborn ewe, however, turned out to be as difficult as starting a secondhand mower. While she would eat anything green, Charlotte did have her preferences; the canes of my mother's raspberries were an especial favorite. I could leave her happily grazing under the elm tree, turn my back for a moment, and then hear my mother shriek, "That sheep is in my raspberry patch!"

I solved the problem by tethering Charlotte, but then found that if I didn't keep moving her, she chewed tight "crop circles" in the lawn and then punctuated them with sheep droppings. And no matter how well I drove her stake into the ground, I'd soon hear my mother shout, "That sheep is in my raspberry patch!"

One time, my mother called me inside to take a telephone call while I was dealing with Charlotte. The 4-H agent had information for me regarding a butterfat milk testing demonstration that I was scheduled to give at the state fair, and as I hurried into the house, I didn't notice that curious Charlotte followed me into the living room. "That sheep is in my house!" my mother shouted.

"Be right back," I told the curious agent on the phone.

Overall, the sheep experiment was less than a success, but we had made a commitment, and what Charlotte lacked in wit she made up for in affection. And to my surprise, she had been with child when I bought her. I named her son Milford and felt like a father. Of sorts.

While my mother liked Milford no more than she cared for Charlotte, my little brother found him an acceptable playmate. Larry would put on a football jersey and shoulder pads to watch football games on TV, and during commercials, he'd run outside with his toy football to enact instant replays with Milford, who found the game delightful. Larry would sprint across the lawn with the lamb in hot pursuit, throw the ball, and then run after Milford and make a flying tackle, throwing the delighted scrambling sheep to the ground.

Unfortunately, Milford took such pleasure in the game that he wanted to play it with everyone. My father and I ignored the sports-minded wooly when he came galloping after us, but not my mother, who was convinced that Milford was the reincarnation of the threatening buck of her childhood.

One day, as Ma was carrying a bucket of hot soapy water across the road from the house to the barn for washing the milking machines, Milford tried to entice her into playing with him. As he joyfully galloped behind her, Mother walked faster and faster, slopping sudsy water in her haste. When she felt her escape was futile, she turned, shouting at Milford, "Go away!" When he made his charge, expecting her to make a flying tackle and wrestle him to the ground, she instead threw the bucket of soapy water on him.

Luckily, the water was not hot enough to cause Milford harm. Only his dignity was injured as he shook himself, looking like a dirty sweater pulled from a basin of Woolite, ready to be rinsed and spread on a towel.

That event spelled doom for my sheep family. As I became more and more involved in campus life, I came home to the farm less and less. Ultimately, I consented; Charlotte and her son were sold down the river, and once I left home, my father bought a riding lawnmower. Used.

A Civil Defense

We can find dark humor in the 1950s drills conducted for school-children in preparation for a possible atomic attack. On command, boys and girls were directed to "duck and cover at the first sign of a flash," crawl beneath their desks, tuck their knees under them, put their faces against the floor, and place their hands over their heads—as one wag said, assuming the perfect position for kissing their asses goodbye.

On Pleasant Ridge, my family took a more informed approach toward dealing with a nuclear disaster. My father became the Willow Township Civil Defense coordinator, and I, a seventh grader, served as his assistant. We attended Civil Defense training sessions in the Richland Center High School gym where, on the shiny wooden floor, representatives of the other townships in the county assembled to hear lectures about scary nuclear disasters, to receive directions on building bomb shelters, and to practice using Geiger counters to detect traces of radiation.

It was serious business, a matter of life and death. We were to serve as the go-to guys for people in our township who had questions about preparing for a nuclear holocaust and surviving should one occur. After we had completed our training, my father and I had the answers, but I don't recall that anyone asked us for information. For most of the nearby farmers, making hay and milking cows seemed more pressing concerns at the time.

But we were ready for the worst. Our house had a full basement, one-half of the space lacking windows. My mother tended
a huge garden, canned throughout the summer season, and stored
her produce on shelves in the cellar: tomatoes and applesauce,
pickles and green beans, corn and even canned beef. Assuming
food would be our biggest obstacle in such a disaster, we would
survive.

Presumably, my father and I would be able to poke our heads
outside and, with the Geiger counter in hand that we had checked
out from the Civil Defense authorities, determine whether or not
it was safe to return to our daily lives on the farm.

We were prepared. We had watched made-for-television nuclear apocalypse movies on *Playhouse 90*. I remember one in particular in which a family had survived because they lived high on
a mountain, thinking they were the only humans left on earth,
but then, after the radioactive ash below had cooled, saw a family
walking toward them, survivors because they had taken shelter in
a mine shaft. With the possibility of this genetic mix, life would
continue on Earth, the boy from one family and the girl from the
other—metaphorically speaking, the next Adam and Eve. Maybe
I'd have that responsibility when I emerged from our basement,
if the Crary girls on the farm to the east had had the foresight to
hide in their basement!

And then I read the end-of-the-world novel *On the Beach*, a
grim scenario in which the United States had been completely
obliterated by an atomic bomb, leaving a radioactive cloud that
slowly drifted west toward Australia. Down under, people were
issued cyanide capsules to ingest for a humane death at the first
sign of radiation sickness. The romantic couple serving as the
Australian protagonists drove up to a lovers' lookout, kissed, and
then, Romeo and Juliet–style, popped their pills. Not for me!
Luckily, we had a snug basement!

Of course, even the people in charge did not completely

understand radiation. Soldiers were issued sunglasses to protect their eyes while they watched atomic test explosions from a "safe" distance. Customers in shoe stores stuck their feet in X-ray machines to check the fit of their new purchases. And the sickly could buy tickets to a small stone cavern in Lone Rock and sit in the presence of low-grade radiation, in search of a cure for whatever ailed them.

The post–World War II generation experienced a life of ambivalence. The United States had emerged the victor in battle, vanquishing the bad guys and enjoying their reward of prosperity. But the complacency that was a part of the 1950s was troubled by worries that the good life would be taken from them, either by Soviet communists who were secretly infiltrating our society (until ferreted out by Senator Joe McCarthy) or the Soviet bombmakers who were planning to blow us to kingdom come (unless we intimidated them by building bigger bombs).

On Pleasant Ridge, a farmer may have grumbled about politics as he leaned against a pickup truck in a neighbor's driveway, but many of them felt they were too busy to even vote, much less worry that Leonard Turnipseed on the lower branch of Buck Creek might be a communist or that some misguided Russian was going to bomb the hell out of their back forty.

My family, though, was prepared. Once the threat had passed, our civil defense shelter that had in an earlier life been only a basement regained its original purpose as a cellar, the Mason jars glistening in the dim light, as un-radioactive as ever. I don't remember when we returned the Geiger counter to the Civil Defense Commission office in Richland Center, but after my parents sold their house to move into town for their retirement, I didn't find it among their belongings. Like the worry of communism and nuclear holocausts, it had disappeared.

But for any of us who have fond memories of that era, vintage Civil Defense Geiger counters are available for sale on eBay.

Hike to Steeple Rock

The month of May was Steeple Rock time back on Pleasant Ridge. I'd hike out across our north forty along the ridge, through the Quackenbush's second growth of woods, until I came to the sandstone formation known to locals as Steeple Rock.

Wind and water erosion, and perhaps the lapping of some ancient sea, had carved five whimsical pillars of stone, each twenty-five to thirty feet in height. Some of the spires interlocked, forming crude Romanesque arches. Others sported little plateaus that enabled climbers to scale them with ease.

Sometimes my brother and sister, parents, or grandparents would accompany me on my annual trek. Other times, I'd take it alone. But regardless of the pilgrimage to the rock, the ritual was unvaried. On the way, we gathered flowers. Most abundant were the delicate blossoms in pastel blues and pinks that my grandparents called mayflowers.

At the rock, the adults rested, admiring but not picking the delicate, lacy-leafed native pasque flowers that grew at the base of the steeples while the young folks clambered about the stone formation. Imagine the feeling of freedom a child experienced standing atop a thirty-foot column of stone, the breeze caressing his body, and a billowy floor of yellow-green treetops at his feet.

Once the adults had caught their breath and the young ones had their fill of scrambling about like so many goats on the rocks, we'd all descend the hill below Steeple Rock to the spring. Pure and icy cold, the water bubbled out of shale and rippled as clear as air over the sand. Hot and tired from the long walk and the play on the rock formation, we'd slurp the delicious water directly from the spring, down on all fours like woodland creatures.

My earliest memory of that spring was when my friend Edna, now long passed, took me there on a walk when I was a child. She and her husband farmed the Quackenbush place at the top of the hill, not far from Steeple Rock.

When my family and I hiked to Steeple Rock, first we drank from the spring—a novelty after our well water—and then we began gathering watercress with its round peppery leaves the size of pennies clustered on tender stems growing directly in the spring bed, the white, threadlike roots securing each plant in the sand. The patches make a dense emerald-green carpet, six to eight inches deep.

We chose watercress that grew nearest the source of the spring, pulling up handfuls and then washing the sand from the roots in the spring water. From my back pocket I pulled plastic bread wrappers and gently coaxed the cress into them. The watercress kept best in the refrigerator as whole plants; it would be carefully sorted and washed right before mealtime, leafy stems broken free from the roots.

Once our bags were full of cress, we began the long, slow ascent up the logging trail that emerged at the gravel lane just below the Quackenbush farmhouse. While this route was slightly longer, it was easier on tired feet than the uneven terrain of the woods. For the next week or so, our salads and especially our sandwiches would be more delicious because of the addition of watercress.

～

One of the nineteenth-century American romantic poets wrote about finding a beautiful seashell on the beach and bringing it home as a souvenir only to find that once it had been moved to another setting, something was missing. So it goes with grocery store watercress.

Not long ago my wife picked up a package as a special treat for me, and I appreciated her thoughtfulness as I made a sandwich of it, white bread slathered with mayonnaise, like the ones I had enjoyed as a kid on the farm. The cress was not as peppery as the fresh cress of my youth, but it conjured images of Granny beside me on her last walk to Steeple Rock, before she became too old to make the journey.

My extended family had just finished a Sunday dinner at our house when, drinking the last of her coffee, Granny announced, "I'm going to walk out to Steeple Rock and pick me some watercress." Her pronouncement was met with silence around the dinner table, as Granny was getting up in years, and always a heavy woman, she had not gotten any lighter with age. "Who'd like to come with me?"

"I'll go with you," I said and immediately went into the kitchen and pulled out the drawer where my mother kept string, paper grocery bags, and plastic bread wrappers. As I stuffed a couple wrappers in my back pocket, I heard my mother say in the other room, "Do you think that's a good idea?"

Granny's answer was to get up from her chair and go into the kitchen. "Got the bags?" she asked. "Good."

And leaving behind the murmuring of adults in the other room, we went out the back door and began our hike to Steeple Rock. It was a glorious day in May, sunny and warm, but not too hot, with a gentle breeze but not a brisk ridge wind. I loved my Granny and savored the idea of spending time alone with her. And as a thirteen-year-old boy who felt that he was coming of age,

I liked the idea of being responsible. Dutifully, I pulled openings between barbed wires in fences and gently put my hand on Granny's back to keep her from snagging her dress as she laboriously clambered through.

Time passed quickly as Granny, invigorated by the adventure, retold stories of her trips to Steeple Rock as a girl. One Easter, she and her friends had taken a picnic that included hard-boiled eggs. Another time, while she and Gramp were courting, he carved their initials in the rock.

The walk out to the crest of the ridge was fairly easy going, but the descent halfway down the hill to the beginning of the outcropping was less so. Granny was not wearing hiking boots, but rather a pair of those old-lady Oxford-style shoes with clunky stacked heels. She had an improvised walking stick in one hand and my hand in the other.

At the rock formation, she found a low ledge to sit on and rest while she tried to remember where Gramp had carved their initials. She pointed to likely spots, but I couldn't find the inscription. Perhaps decades of wind and rain and ice had erased the declaration of love.

The descent from the rock to the spring was worrisome for me, as Granny was obviously still tired. Should we take a longer route with a more gradual decline, or should we move extra slowly and extra carefully down the shorter steep grade? Ultimately, I sorted out a compromise, and we made the descent safely to the spring. Granny lacked the agility to hunker down and slurp from the spring as I did, so instead she bent over at the waist and scooped up water in her cupped hands.

She caught her breath while I harvested a bag of cress for her and then another for my family. Then I took both bags in one hand and Granny's hand in the other as we began our difficult and treacherous ascent. When I asked her which return route she preferred, she opted for the shorter option, up the hill. As we started up, both of us occasionally grasping saplings for support, I wondered if she had made the correct decision, but now we were committed.

When we had made it as far as the rock and Granny declared she needed to rest, I felt a strong sense of dread. Would she be able to make it up the hill? What in the world would I do if she couldn't?

After a lengthy rest, we continued on, Granny determined to make it to the top before she rested again. And she did, leaning on her walking stick as she paused, breathing so hard at first that she didn't want to talk. Finally, she said, "I'm so pooped I'd like to sit down in the grass." She laughed. "But I probably couldn't get up again!"

Finally, we continued on, my heart thumping not from exertion but from anxiety. What had I gotten us into? How could I be such a stupid kid! What if Granny had a heart attack? I furtively swiped tears from my eyes so that Granny couldn't see them. Whenever we stopped to rest, I'd try to calculate mentally how far we had gone and how much farther we had to go, grateful when I determined we had passed the halfway point. An overwhelming sense of relief flooded over me when I could see our house in the distance.

We had made it.

"How was the walk?" my father asked as we entered the living room and Granny plopped herself in a rocker.

"It was good!" she said. "But I'm pooped! Is there any more coffee?"

"I'll get you some," I volunteered.

"The percolator's still plugged in," my mother said. "But it'll be pretty strong."

Granny laughed. "I don't want to have to drink a barrel of water to get a little coffee. Bring me a cup!"

In Gramp's Shoes

"You look just like him," my second cousin said, pointing at the image of my grandfather. Gramp was pictured standing in a row of relatives in one of the old photographs that she had copied and brought to my uncle's ninetieth birthday party.

"No," I said, frowning, staring at the short, skinny, forty-something guy in the snapshot that I held in my hand. "I don't see it at all."

"I do," my wife said, taking the photo from me and studying it carefully.

"Thanks," I scoffed, assuming that she was teasing me. Gramp had not been my favorite grandparent, as she well knew.

"No," she said, seriously. "I can see a family resemblance."

My Granny had been a favorite, probably because she had cared for me when I was a baby while my mother had gone back to teaching. In many respects, she was like a second mother, only far more indulgent. I was the first of her grandchildren, and I always hoped that I was her favorite even after her total number of grandkids reached six.

She had been a large and pillowy woman who liked rocking chairs. Her hair had been pure white for as long as I could remember, regularly permed into a halo of white frizz. She wore a house dress, her hankie tucked inside the bodice within easy reach. Every time I sat in her lap, I felt that she had been custom designed for my comfort.

I am told that when I was a little boy and she would visit our farm, she'd walk around the lawn, her hands clasped behind her back, checking out the flowering shrubs and perennial beds. I'd follow a few steps behind, my hands held behind my back in imitation of hers.

But I felt no such affinity for Gramp. When I was a toddler, I once opened the door to their icebox and took out the butter, which I held in my hands and examined with curiosity.

"Give that to me!" Gramp commanded.

In fear of his retribution, I threw it in his direction with all my might, where it landed, short of its destination, in a flop on the linoleum floor. That misadventure, unfortunately, set a tone for our relationship.

～

When my mother was assembling the clothing that I would wear for my eighth grade graduation ceremony, an occasion when graduates from one-room schools all over the county assembled at the Richland Center High School gymnasium to receive their diplomas, Gramp announced, "Gary can borrow my shoes so you won't have to buy him a pair. We're the same size. He'd just outgrow new ones anyway."

As Gramp and I both wore a men's size 6 shoe, technically his fit me. But he had short wide adult feet while mine were the slender growing feet of a boy. I had to pull the laces extra tight and still felt as if I were walking with webbed duck feet. But the sports coat that my mother had ordered from the JC Penney catalog was new, as was my clip-on bow tie. I could tolerate the shoes.

Now the loan of Gramp's footwear seems more than an indication of his waste not, want not penury. In retrospect, his desire to put me in his shoes seems both literal and metaphorical. Both of Gramp's sons had become farmers like him. And like him, he wanted me to be a farmer, too.

Sometimes it felt as if he were trying to physically shape me, like God molding Adam from clay. Whenever he thought the fingernails of his young grandson were too long, he'd pull me onto his lap, reach into his pocket for the jackknife, one that he used to peel apples, make willow branch whistles, and "fix" little boy pigs, and then pare my fingernails. My protests were in vain. Although the fingernail-cutting was more like an enhanced interrogation technique than a manicure, my parents insisted that I sit still and submit. I squirmed until Gramp would scold, "Jee-shus Kee-ryest, stop squirming!"

Gramp also announced that he would cut my hair, saving my parents the expense of taking me to a barbershop. He had a pair of manual hair clippers that worked on the principle of grass shears and required a steadier hand than Gramp's. Intuitively, he felt that a gentle tug of the handles along with the squeeze that closed the blades was necessary for the clippers to do their job, and as I protested "Ow!" whenever he pulled my hair, he'd shout, "Jee-shus Kee-ryest, sit still!"

Gramp had one hairstyle in his barbering repertoire: skinned on the back and sides with a cockatoo crest, a farmer's haircut.

Eventually, my parents excused me from Gramp's home-style haircuts. I suspect that I had gained an ally in my father, as no doubt he had been subjected to the same tonsorial regimen when he was my age.

For my thirteenth birthday, Gramp presented me with a safety razor. I thanked him politely, as I had been taught, but I had nothing on my face to shave. True, I was about to start high school, but my mother had enrolled me in first grade when I was five, and I was not early to mature. I kept the razor on my dresser, waiting for the day when whiskers would finally begin sprouting on my chin.

Gramp's attempts to groom me for farming were no more successful than his attempt to groom me physically. He had encouraged me to cut weeds in the cow pasture, hoping to instill in me a love of the land, a less than successful approach to nurturing an agrarian sensibility. He lamented the fact that I didn't enjoy farm machinery, that I at best tolerated milking time, and that in general, I showed little interest in farming.

Once, when I closed a barbed wire gate ("bob" wire gate, as Gramp would say) by putting the top of the gatepost into the wire loop before the bottom, he made me start over, insisting that I put the post in bottom first. "That is the proper way to close a gate," he announced, pointing an accusatory finger at me.

When he used his all-purpose jackknife to cut tufts of hay missed by the mower, he returned my stare of incredulity with a look of smug self-righteousness. "Anything worth doing," he proclaimed, "is worth doing well."

Gramp, who was a nonsmoker, ironically developed emphysema when he was in his early fifties, a time when the only treatment was rest and wintering in the Southwest. But during the summer, he put on appropriate farmer attire and left the flat that he and Granny rented in town to arrive at our house by seven in the morning to supervise farming operations during the day.

He was generous with his advice as to when the weather was right for planting corn or cutting hay. He could spot-check to be certain that a cow had indeed been milked dry. He was quick to point out when a Sunday picnic should be canceled in favor of making hay because the following week might be rainy.

Neither Gramp nor my father had attended school beyond the eighth grade, and Gramp remained unconvinced as to the value of my high school education. To persuade him otherwise, I attempted to explain negative numbers, a concept I was learning in freshman algebra. He dismissed algebra in general, and our

discussion became heated to the point that Granny called me out
of the room and scolded me not to argue with him.

Slowly, though, he seemed to come to terms with the fact that
I would choose my own path and that the path would take me far
beyond Pleasant Ridge.

"You're not going to farm, are you?" he said to me one time
when my family was visiting him and my grandmother.

Silently, I shook my head.

"I thought so," he said, his voice grim with resignation.

I shrugged and quietly left the room.

∾

After I came of age, I learned not to take Gramp too seriously. My
family had let him rule the roost like a feisty banty rooster, but
I came to realize that they might be making allowances for his
poor health. And while he may have been an OCD personality,
his mother-in-law had recognized his sense of responsibility and
chose him rather than one of her shiftless sons to take over her
late husband's farm.

The pattern of sons taking over their father's land has for the
most part come to an end on the ridge, because many of the sons,
like me, left to earn a college degree in hopes of gaining a more
affluent livelihood. Now the remaining dairy farmers survive by
increasing their acreage, their herd size, and the sophistication of
their machinery. When a farmer retires or dies, his land is generally purchased by another farmer and his house occupied either
by someone who works in town or by a city person who uses it
as a summer home in the country.

My younger brother tried farming when he first graduated
from high school, but he too left for the greener pastures of a
job in the city. At that point, our father decided to sell the farm,
and I found that even from my city digs, I still felt the pull of
the land. I decided to buy half of the 180 acres on a fifteen-year

land contract, explaining to my wife that I was making a double investment, one financial, as prices for farmland were low at the time, and the second, emotional. Gramp had already passed away, but if he were keeping his customary watchful eye on the farm from heaven, I knew he would be pleased that part of the land had remained in the family, even if I had chosen not to "pull tits and shovel shit" as a dairy farmer.

And later, after my wife and I had become resigned to a life without grandchildren, our forty-year-old daughter announced that she was pregnant, and we became the grandparents of a sweet little girl. When my wife and I talked about what we wanted Julia to call us, I surprised myself by the name that immediately came to me. "I want her to call me Gramp," I told my wife.

And so I became Gramp. I not only wore his shoes to my eighth-grade graduation, but in a familial sense, I still do. And just as Gramp pampered my little sister, I am devoted to Julia, indulging her shamelessly.

While I am still irritated when I remember our prior inter-actions, I understand him better. From his time as a World War I soldier through his long siege with emphysema, he carried with him a sense of his own mortality and a belief that only through family and land does a farmer endure. Gramp may have been a sonofabitch, but I see more and more of him in myself.

After all, he was my grandfather.

Farm Forecasts

Back on the farm, we didn't need a TV weather forecaster to tell us when it was going to rain. Pleasant Ridge folks knew to look for all sorts of signs the weather was going to change.

Animals seemed to sense an incoming storm, and an observant farmer became privy to their insight. Dark clouds were sure to appear if starlings flew in circles, or if frogs down in the valley crossed the road, or if dogs and cats ate grass. And whenever a bobwhite chirped to his flock, his call may have sounded like *bobwhite, bobwhite* to the untrained, but to the ridge farmers he warned, "More wet, more wet."

Natural clues abound, all certain signs of approaching precipitation. No overnight dew on the grass meant rain the next day. Gramp Jones maintained that leaves turned out or upside down on a tree announced showers were on their way. A circle around the moon indicated a storm, and a count of the stars within that halo determined the number of days before the first drops fell. And old-timers recognized a "rainy moon," a new moon tipped up allowing water to run out, a sign of a wet month.

You might know the rhyme, "Red sky in the morning, farmer's fair warning; red sky at night, farmer's delight." While ridge dwellers paid special heed to this admonition, they supplemented it with other conditional forecasts. For example, when the fog went up, the rain without question would come down. If the sun set clear on Friday night, then it would rain three days out of the coming week. A rainstorm on Easter meant rain on the following seven Sundays.

And then Paw claimed he was a rainmaker who could bring on precipitation any time he chose. All he had to do was mow hay. Farmwives have their signs of coming changes in the weather, too. Potatoes often boiled dry when rain was in the air. Moisture beaded on pipes and water tanks. Both the radio and the telephone crackled before a storm. And, of course, Granny Jones's arthritis suddenly flared up, the surest sign of all.

My mother vowed that she could outdo my father as a rainmaker. If hanging the wash outside on a clothesline didn't bring rain, inviting company for Sunday dinner certainly would.

Ridge folks had a number of ways to predict dry weather, too. For instance, if we woke up to rain, we'd automatically recite, "Rain before seven, quit before eleven." On some hot summer nights, heat lightning flashed in the sky. "Forked lightning at night, next day bright," Paw asserted. And dusty whirlwinds, Cousin Verne insisted, were a sign of a coming dry season, as were "spotty rains," cloudbursts that fell on localized areas.

As a conversation opener, old Otto Fry would mourn after church, "I wish it'd rain. We sure could use rain." Paw never agreed. "Dry weather will scare a farmer to death, but wet weather will starve him to death," he said, remembering those years when rain kept him out of the fields. During a rainy spell, Paw would storm about, slipping through mud in the barnyard, cursing and bellowing, "I hope Otto Fry is sucking this mud up his—" er, never mind.

Perhaps my father's petulant vulgarity might be partially excused by his dependence on good weather for successful farming. Crops couldn't be planted in muddy fields if a spring was too wet. Corn couldn't be cultivated during a rainy summer, nor hay cut. And mowed hay needed to dry for a few days in the sun before it was brought into the barn. Likewise, oats were shocked and again left in the field until threshing time. And corn couldn't be picked during wet fall seasons.

Maybe folk forecasts on the ridge weren't always accurate. But they were certainly more colorful than those of a scientist working with dry data and pointing at computer mockups projected on a screen. And even with today's marvels of advanced meteorological technology, sometimes professionals have to eat humble pie.

As the son of a farmer, I still maintain a wary eye for signs of changing weather. When I step outside the front door of my summer place in Door County, if I feel a breeze coming out of the east over Lake Michigan, I nod sagely and tell myself, "Rain is on the way."

The Grasshopper

Ostensibly, my father bought Frank Brewer's Farmall F-12 for me to use cultivating corn. I was a young teenager with an extremely modest mechanical aptitude. In retrospect, I suspect that the tractor was to serve as my training wheels before I was allowed to operate more complex machinery. If I remember correctly, my father paid seventy-five dollars for the tractor; if I had wrecked it, we wouldn't have been out much money.

My father decided that I would drive the tractor up the Dicks Hill from Frank's place on Double D to where it junctioned with County D and then continue on to our farm, a total distance of about a mile and a half. With coaching, Frank standing on one side of me and my father on the other, I started the tractor, no small feat, as it had a crank at the front like a Model T.

As I mounted and sat in the hole-dotted tin seat, Frank gave me instructions on braking and shifting, my father observing the lesson. I knew how to drive our family's tractor, so I was fairly confident that I could manage this antique version. All seemed to be going well as I drove along the edge of the fence row toward the gate that opened onto the gravel road—when without warning, as if it had a mind of its own, the F-12 veered sharply to the left, crashing through the brush and plummeting over the bank into the ditch.

Frank and Paw ran to survey the damage I had caused while I

remained seated on the F-12, overcome with guilt at my ineptness in maneuvering it. I felt only slightly better when an investigation revealed that sheared bolts in the linkage connecting the steering wheel with the front wheels had caused the accident, not my driving incompetence.

The two men soon replaced the bolts and extricated the tractor from the ditch, set the brake, and left it out of gear on the road, the motor running. Like a cowboy who dutifully remounts the horse that had thrown him, I climbed back on the F-12 and began my maiden journey up the Dicks Hill.

The ancient tractor had metal rear wheels with cleats that made the vehicle vibrate like a Magic Fingers mattress on the gravel road, a bone-jarring, tooth-rattling ride, but I made the trip home with no further complications. By the time I pulled into our driveway, I had named the steel exhaust-breathing beast the Grasshopper.

We had an uneasy alliance that summer, the Grasshopper and I, following countless rows of field corn back and forth. The turns were challenging, and inevitably I'd plow out a few plants, climb down, and reset them, crossing my fingers and hoping for the best. On the tedious straightaways, I'd pull a dime-store harmonica from my pocket and practice tunes I could play by ear: "Red River Valley," "Oh, Susanna," and "My Old Kentucky Home."

I took off my shirt, envisioning the healthy tan of the beach-combing bullies who kicked sand in the eyes of the ninety-pound weaklings like me, scrawny kids who had not yet signed up for the mail-order Charles Atlas bodybuilding course advertised in comic books.

By the day's end, my back would be seared a bright red and I'd have to climb into bed carefully that night and sleep only on my stomach, my back uncovered. A few days later, I would pull translucent patches of skin off my back, secure in the folk wisdom of the time that peeling skin was a necessary step on the way to a healthy dark tan. The specter of skin cancer didn't rear its fearsome head until I was no longer a barefoot boy with cheeks of tan but an old man with suspicious spots on my back that a dermatologist spritzed with liquid nitrogen.

Despite my on-the-job training on the Grasshopper, I was never asked to bale hay or plow fields, to plant corn or sow oats, or even to spread manure. I was the Miniver Cheevy of farm life, born too late and in the wrong place. I would no doubt have been happy on one of those eighty-acre farmsteads located on Si Breese Lane, on a first name basis with a team of work horses, Dick and Ned, and a cart horse, Maud.

Perhaps my father sensed the obsolete temperament in me when he purchased that bit of farming antiquity, the F-12, as a compromise. But despite his attempt to entice me into an agrarian way of life, I counted the days until I could leave the farm behind me, like the sunburns that peeled my skin.

And the Grasshopper stayed behind, too, moved back behind the corn crib after I left for college, its presence soon obscured in a grove of saplings. My father had planned to restore the F-12 as a retirement project, but when he sold the home place and moved to town, he took with him only his maul. As far as I know, the Grasshopper still rusts in peace on Pleasant Ridge in the obscurity of a second-growth grove of trees.

Milking Time

"I love to go swimmin', with bow-legged women, and dive between their legs!" my father sang as we were doing the nightly milking. I was too innocent then to understand the double entendre and too young to do more than help with the chores, like washing the cows' udders before they were milked. After my father had emptied the milking machine into a pail, it was my job to carry the bucket to the end of the center driveway to the milk cans I had brought in from the milk house. Carefully, I dumped the pail of milk through the milk strainer into a can.

We milked at most twenty-two cows with two milking machines, a task that took a couple hours, including preparation and cleanup. The morning and evening chores were relentless, even when my father had succumbed to a morning malady my mother called idiot's flu, the result of spending Saturday night at a tavern in the nearby village Hub City.

Under the best of circumstances, mind-numbing repetition and endless waiting made the work boring. Paw and I sought diversion in any quarter that presented itself.

One of our fantasies was to sell the cows and use the profit to buy a house trailer for wintering in Florida. But we couldn't take Ma, Paw cautioned me, because "the bathing beauties would hurt her eyes."

Like playing cowboys and Indians with my friends, such fantasies seemed stimulating but harmless. I considered my father's fanciful scenario—featuring bathing beauties but not my mother—with the quiet acceptance of a young boy. I knew from experience that Ma was deathly afraid of water, fearful that if she waded up to her waist, she might develop a cramp and drown; of course, she wouldn't want to join us, but we would eventually return to her.

When my father retired and sold his herd of milk cows, rather than traveling to Florida, he chose an over-fifty trailer park in south Texas, featuring a bevy of elderly women and an above-ground pool, neither of which seemed to bother my mother.

～

When Paw was a student at Pleasant Ridge School, memorizing poetry was an integral part of the curriculum, and perhaps because he had not cluttered his mind with education beyond the eighth grade, the poems stayed with him. As he moved milking machines and I dumped buckets of milk, he'd recite Longfellow's "The Village Blacksmith," Edward R. Sill's "Opportunity," Walt Whitman's "O Captain! My Captain!," and a piece with so much internal rhyme that it was a challenge to recite:

Amidst the mists and coldest frosts
With stoutest wrists and loudest boasts
He thrusts his fists against the post
And still insists he sees the ghosts.

Research offers no author for this verse, other than calling it a folk nursery rhyme and an old tongue-twister sometimes used as an articulation exercise.

Ironically, while I, too, was required to memorize poems in

grade school—an easy task for me—I remember none of them, but I can still recite fragments of the poems I learned by listening to my father while we were milking cows.

However, Paw's grade school poems were not the only pieces I committed to memory in the barn. As I fantasized about a future career as an actor, I auditioned for high school plays and competed in forensics. When I had a monologue or a role in a play to memorize, I took my script with me to the barn and recited the dialog as I washed cow udders and dumped pails of milk. My script always smelled of cow manure.

After morning milking when I was getting ready for school, I'd take a "spit bath," standing shirtless at the bathroom sink and wiping myself clean with a wet, soapy washcloth. Sometimes at school I'd notice the mingled smell of cow manure and grass silage on the inside of my wrist.

But I didn't hold that smell against the cows. The barn in winter was actually a pleasant environment. The body heat of our herd kept the barn basement relatively temperate, not T-shirt warm, but jacket warm. And I enjoyed the yeasty aroma of silage and the herbal scent of hay. Even the earthy odor of fresh cow dung, with its vegetable base, wasn't an unpleasant smell, although admittedly it may have been an acquired appreciation.

And while I disliked the monotonous routine of milking, I actually was fond of the cows. Because we spent a great deal of time with them, we became acquainted with their individual personalities, and those who were affectionate and cooperative were our favorites. Each one had a name. The most memorable was Mary Belle, a dairy animal that had long outlived her peak of milk production. If my father had been a more business-minded farmer, she would have long ago been sold, but truth be told, we loved her. She ambled slowly outside when released from her stanchion and walked even more slowly on her return. Her spot was adjacent to the walkway leading to the silo, and each time I passed her, I petted her shoulder and she would turn her head to look at me appreciatively.

⌒

My father's barn secret was the fact that he had named his cows after the women on the ridge. While that might make him sound like a misogynist, he wasn't; no insult to the ladies of the neighborhood was intended.

One time, when I was feeling impish, I told my father's first cousin Marjory that we had a cow named after her. Without missing a beat, she looked me in the eye and replied with all seriousness, "Really? Well, we have a pig named Gary." Now, that insult was probably intended.

When I was in high school, we kept a radio plugged into a light socket on an improvised shelf in the barn basement. When the lights were on, the radio played, not because we thought, like some dairy herdsmen, that music improved milk production, but because the tunes helped to relieve boredom. WRCO in Richland Center was our local station for news in the morning and for popular music in the evening. The night program accepted requests if they were submitted on a postcard. With my adolescent sense of humor, I requested a song—the tune now long forgotten—for twenty-two girls with whom I spent time before school in the morning and after supper at night.

My boyish funny bone was tickled, too, when our barn cats experienced elimination problems. We used gauze filter pads in the large funnel-like strainer through which we filtered milk. When we finished milking, I'd toss the used filter pad to the barn cats, and the one that caught it would wolf it down for the residual milk. Unfortunately, the pad would sometimes not pass smoothly through the feline's gastrointestinal tract. I would lend not a helping hand, but a foot, stepping on the part of the filter that had thus far emerged, and hissing, "Scat!"

Less amusing were the times we'd come out to the barn in the morning and find that a cow had prematurely given birth to her calf while she was restrained by her stanchion and her newborn delivered into the "drop," the gutter designed to catch and collect the cows' waste until the daily barn cleaning. The calf would be coated with excrement, and the window for the cow's instinct to lick her newborn clean would have closed. We'd wipe the pathetic wobbly legged youngster with gunnysacks, knowing it would never be clean until the eventual growth of a new coat of hair.

And sometimes the cow would not let her calf suckle. Either my father or I would have to stand behind her holding her tail erect, as then she would not move, and her baby would be able to nurse. Eventually, she'd accept her newborn.

Frightening were the times when we had summer storms before the haymow was full, and the empty barn would sway and creak like a ship without ballast in a hurricane at sea. But even more terrifying were the moments when one of us would look out the kitchen window toward the barn and think the building had caught fire, the heart palpitations finally subsiding with the realization that a light had been inadvertently left on inside the barn or that the glow was nothing but a reflected sunset.

I came of age milking cows, eventually developing the strength to carry a full milk can out to the milk house and hoist it over the rim of the tank to cool in well water. I developed the skill and maturity to milk cows by myself, my father confident that I had done a good job. And I understood more clearly the delicate balance between the sensibilities of farmwives and the coarser nature of their husbands.

But more important, I came to the realization that operating a dairy farm was not going to be my calling after I graduated from college. The time for me to milk was coming to an end.

Making Hay While the Sun Shines

Two of my earliest memories deal with making hay. One of them was riding down our hill sitting on the hayrack as the tractor pulled it along the road to the hundred acres during the haying season. With my legs dangling over the edge of the rack, my fingers laced in the grooves between the boards on the bed, and my head tipped back in the breeze, I felt as if I were flying when my father took the tractor out of gear and let gravity accelerate our trip.

The other vivid image I have is of the daily summer picnics under the four pines on our front lawn during the haying season. As the hours were long on days we made hay, everyone stopped for a lunch midway between our noontime dinner and evening supper. My mother often made summer sausage sandwiches with chocolate chip cookies for dessert, a pitcher of iced tea for the grownups and Kool-Aid for the kids. Gramp and Uncle Vern joined my family sitting on a blanket in the shade, snacking and resting before returning to the hot fields and haymow.

I loved haying when I was a boy, finding it almost as exciting as threshing. In addition to the fields over on the hundred, we had cropland both to the north of the house on one side of the road and to the south of the barn on the other. Farms that crested the spine of the ridge were of necessity broken up, separated by pastures and woodlots on hills and valleys too steep for tilling, the inevitable landscape of Driftless topography. The trips to the barn were tense as we worried that precarious loads of loose hay might slide off before we reached our destination, but the return trip to the field was one of joyous, rapid abandon.

More than a half century has passed since I left the farm, and the machinery that we used during my childhood is now relegated to rural farm life museums. When I was very young, my family was transitioning from our horses to an 8N Ford tractor and subsequently continued to use the implements once drawn by draft horses, but now by tractor horsepower.

Today on country roads, I see gigantic farm machinery that may have sold new for six figures, its purpose sometimes a mystery to me. With air-conditioned cabs, the equipment resembles set pieces for a remake of *War of the Worlds* rather than the simple hay mowers, rakes, and loaders of my childhood, their mechanism powered by gears connected to the movement of wheels as a horse or tractor pulled them.

Farmers listened to weather reports and studied the sky, looking for signs of coming bad weather before mowing hay, as it had to lie in the sun and dry for a couple of days before it could be raked into windrows. If rain fell on the raked hay before it could be taken into the barn, then the hay was tedded, a raking process with the tines reversed to spread the hay until it had dried and could be re-raked.

The hay-loader was a primitive elevator that was pulled behind the hay wagon. Loose hay dropped onto the flatbed where a farmer had the dusty job of stacking it with a three-tined hayfork, wading through and tramping on the hay as he worked. Many times, that man would ride atop the load as it was hauled to the barn. I treasure an old black-and-white photograph of my father as a young man standing atop a wagonload of hay, reins in his hands as he drives Dick and Ned to the barn in the background.

If driving the load of hay to the barn was a precarious trip, raising it into the barn with a hayfork was even more of a challenge.

High up in the peak of the barn rafters, an iron track ran from one end to the other. During haying, the bottom-hinged door at one end of the peak was lowered. A hemp hay rope was threaded through pulleys at both ends of the track, one end attached to the double-tined harpoon hayfork that was plunged into a pile of loose hay on the wagon, the other end attached to horses, or later, a tractor. I remember my mother sometimes being pressed into service to drive our 8N Ford when my grandfather wasn't available.

The pulley mechanism carried each load of hay up to the peak, where it traveled along the track until someone inside the haymow shouted for the trip rope to be pulled and the hay dropped into the appropriate mow.

At least, that was how the process was supposed to work. Sometimes the forked hay would fall loose before it reached the peak of the barn, and the fork would be reloaded.

The work of stacking the hay in the mow, again with a three-tined hayfork, was the most difficult work of all and usually fell to my father. Walking in loose hay was like wading through deep mud, and the summer temperatures soared in the haymow. When my father emerged from the mow once a load of hay had been stacked, chafe clung to his sweaty face, making him look like an actor in one of the tasteless minstrel shows that were popular at the time.

Just as over time we transitioned from horses to mechanical horsepower, our tractors became larger and our machinery more complex. My father purchased a used Allis-Chalmers baler that with a series of rotating belts was supposed to produce hay rolled into small round bales. Sometimes it worked efficiently, after my father had cursed and hammered and welded broken parts.

By age twelve, I could drive tractor on the hay wagon while my father and uncle, wearing leather gloves and using hay hooks, loaded the bales. I would spot four-leaf clovers (as could my

Granny Jones), and I would call to my uncle and point when I saw one. He would patiently pick it for me, and I'd hold the bouquet of four-leaf clovers until we returned to the house, where I'd put them in a jelly glass of water until I had time to press them in an encyclopedia and eventually tape them into a scrapbook.

The round bales were fed into the haymow using an elevator operated with the power take-off of the tractor. My father still had to stack them in the barn.

The used square baler that replaced the other was far less temperamental, and by the time it arrived on the scene, I was strong enough to load hay bales as they were popped onto the wagon flatbed. My parents praised my ability to efficiently load bales that invariably arrived safely stowed to the barn, where I lifted them onto the elevator and my father stacked them in the haymow. Not until I was much older did I realize that they were probably using flattery to keep me working during the hay season for a very modest weekly allowance.

By the time I graduated from college and married, effectively retiring from making hay, my father used a baler that produced small square bales, pitching them into a basket-style hayrack. Because of their relatively small size, they were allowed to fall from the elevator into the haymow and were left where they lay with minimal stacking. In preparation for baling, a single machine mowed, crimped, and windrowed the hay, minimizing the drying time.

And now the giant round bales, forklifted into sheds or wrapped in plastic to be left in the fields, are nearly as big as our first 8N Ford tractor.

～

The barn, built at the turn of the twentieth century, no longer stands on the farm where I helped make hay. When my father stopped farming, he did not want the building to deteriorate until it tumbled to the ground and began decomposing. In a sense, he euthanized it. Before he pulled the whole thing down and burned the remains, my mother took a picture of the structure and saved one of the stones from the basement for me.

These artifacts help preserve the barn in my memory, where it still looms large—especially the haymow. I remember milking cows during early summer storms before the hay season and hearing the empty haymow swaying and creaking dangerously in the wind. And I remember climbing up the ladder of the hay chute during the winter into an icy, cavernous, churchlike silence, occasionally interrupted by the cooing of pigeons roosting on the old hay track, and throwing down bales for the dairy herd. In the barn's milking parlor, the heat generated by the bodies of the cows made the milking parlor seem toasty by contrast.

And I remember my father climbing—I was astonished at his quiet courage. I could never climb the outside of the windmill to adjust the television antenna, scale the outside of the silo to attach the silage blower pipe, or creep up the ladder inside the empty haymow to thread the hemp rope through the hayfork pulley on the track under the roof peak.

I didn't realize until much later just how difficult this had been for him.

After Paw had retired from farming and making hay, he and my mother visited my family in Door County, and I took him to climb the famous Peninsula State Park tower. Only a quarter of the way up the stairs, he stopped.

"Are you tired?" I asked him.

"No," he said. "I'm afraid."

"Afraid?" I asked him incredulously.

"Yeah," he said, softly. "I don't have to climb anymore."

Threshing on the Ridge

"A barrel of salt and an extension table is all I need to feed threshers," Hattie Bryant once claimed. If that doesn't make any sense to you, don't worry. A lot of what Hattie said wasn't particularly cogent, but folks back on Pleasant Ridge liked her anyway. And coping with the challenge of feeding twenty-man threshing crews was something that all the farmwomen had in common.

Fred Pauls owned the threshing machine. When farmers had cut and shocked their oats, usually between the end of July and the last part of August, the threshing season began.

Fred charged four cents a bushel for use of the machine that separated grain from chaff and straw, and the men exchanged help along with the use of their tractors and wagons. Likewise, the wives assisted each other in preparing the tremendous meals required to feed the hungry crews.

Early in the season, my mother began planning her menu. My father planted enough oats that she knew the threshers would be present for at least two meals. Each night when my father returned home from the day's threshing, she asked what he had been served for dinner and supper and his best guess when the threshers would arrive at our farm.

These were important questions, because a farmwife wanted to be certain not only that everything was ready for the threshers but also that she avoided duplicating an earlier menu. She would feel that she had disgraced herself if she learned that because of her inattention, the men had had roast beef and apple pie two days in a row.

While feeding threshers was a challenging undertaking for the farmwives, it was also something to look forward to, a chance to get together with some neighbor women and to show off their homes and their culinary specialties.

Timing the meal was always a problem. A woman couldn't kill her chickens or get the frozen beef from the locker plant in town too far in advance. So many variables could alter the scheduled threshing date—the weather, mechanical breakdowns, or maybe Fred Pauls's changes in plans.

One day, many years ago, my grandmother's afternoon rest in her rocker was disturbed by the sound of footsteps, and she awoke to find Fred on her porch, laughing ruefully at the last-minute imposition. "I guess you're having threshers for supper," he said.

Granny did some fast thinking and even faster moving. She opened some jars of her home-canned beef, threw together some pies, and peeled a bucket of potatoes. The meal was ready on time.

My mother liked to serve fried chicken, one of her specialties. Every spring she purchased baby chicks at Pulvermacher's Produce in Richland Center, and the young roosters would be ready for slaughter by threshing time. If she chose a different meal option, Fred would protest, "Esther! Why didn't you cook up some chicken?"

Mother knew that the men always enjoyed eating her meals. One woman on the ridge, though, was a notoriously bad cook, and the crew tried to avoid eating at her place if at all possible. Her house was none too clean, the cream sometimes soured, and the meat sometimes tainted. Once she reportedly served an infamous meal of undercooked boiled chicken with kernels of corn from the bird's craw floating in the broth.

When the threshing day had been established with some

degree of certainty, I was sent to the range house out in the field where the young fryers were kept to snatch Mother's unsuspecting victims. Six or eight of the birds were required to make a threshing meal. As the sun sank, my father chopped off their heads, and my mother scalded them and plucked steaming handfuls of soggy feathers. By bedtime, the refrigerator was filled with cut-up chicken ready for frying.

The next morning, our farm was electric with excitement. We kids found that for drama, threshing was an event surpassed only by the county fair. I helped knock down the shocks of oats so that the bundles could dry from the dew in the early morning sun. Soon, tractors and wagons began arriving on the road, our dog greeting each with hysterical yelping.

Finally that behemoth, the grand old thresher, slowly lumbered into the barnyard, creaking and rattling, in retrospect looking like a robotic dinosaur. While the machine was being set up, the men began loading bundles of oats onto the basket racks of their wagons. Ordinarily, farming was a solitary occupation, the men finding rare opportunities to talk to each other while leaning against a pickup truck in a neighbor's driveway or during a chance encounter at the grist mill. My father used to joke that his only contact with the outside world was when the mailman made his delivery at the roadside mailbox. But during threshing, men could enjoy conversations as they worked, at least when they were not standing next to the factorylike roar of the thresher.

Once a wagon was loaded with fork-pitched bundles of oats, a driver brought it to the thresher where the bundles were pitched into the machine. The oats were separated from the straw, which was blown into a crescent-shaped pile by the moving arm of the blower.

My father was often the stacker, not only for our threshing but for that of our neighbors, work for which he was paid. Wading through the straw, he stacked it with a three-tined fork and packed it with his feet while perspiring profusely. Chaff and dust clung to his face as well as to his sweat-soaked shirt.

From another pipe extending from the thresher, a stream of oats spewed into the bed of a pickup truck. At the granary, more men shoveled the oats into an elevator that dropped them into the building again to be shoveled into place.

While threshing could be dirty and noisy work, for those out in the fields, the task was relatively relaxing—the bundles light, the summer air warm and pleasant, and the male camaraderie much appreciated. Far from the earshot of the women, the guys felt they could let their rough edges show.

They could brag about their tractors' comparative horsepower and recall teams of horses they remembered from their younger days. They could show off their strength and demonstrate their fitness by standing in a round-bottomed metal bushel basket, lofting a gunnysack of oats onto their shoulders. They could boast of fistfights won, like the time one farmer at a tavern in Hub City punched an obnoxious drunken veterinarian in the nose (never mind that the assailant's friends had to take up a collection to pay his fine when the vet brought charges).

Like their wives, they gossiped about sexual matters, one guy laughing about the time he and his wife-to-be enjoyed alfresco intimate relations, only to learn later that they had bedded down in a patch of poison ivy. Another guy told of a farmer who had forgiven his unfaithful wife. "I wouldn't take her back," the gossiping farmer said, "if she'd board herself and drink at the creek!" And they could tell off-color jokes, usually one about a farmer's daughter and a traveling salesman.

In short, farmers enjoyed the novelty of a comfortable communal experience, a freedom to be as crude as they wanted without offending the ears of their womenfolk. Then again, maybe the women enjoyed their own chance to talk freely while preparing the meal inside.

The pies were the first order of business. At least five or six were required, and of course, there must be at least two kinds. My grandmother, my mother's best friend Dorothy, and Aunt JoAnn helped. Granny usually took charge of the lemon pies, her specialty.

One of the women had to start peeling potatoes; it took ten to fifteen pounds for one meal. Someone had to chop the cabbage for slaw. Someone else dished up the jelly and jam and the pickles. The baked beans were already in the oven, and the dough for rolls had to be shaped into buns.

As the men loved homemade noodles with chicken, Mother often made them. To produce a sufficient quantity, she used a dozen eggs and as many cups of flour and tablespoons of cream. The quickest way to cook the chicken was to brown it in frying pans and then finish it up in the pressure cooker, especially if it was served with noodles. Heating up the vegetable, usually canned corn, was last-minute work, as was starting the coffee in Dorothy Johnson's huge percolator.

Not all the work took place in the hot kitchen. The living room was transformed into a dining room, with the table extended to its maximum length. Mother's best tablecloth and dishes were spread on it. The room, along with the entire house, was sparkling clean. Because a woman's reputation as a homemaker was on the line at threshing time, the special housecleaning had begun weeks earlier.

Outside by the pump, the washtub of water had been warming slowly in the sun. Before lunch, a teakettle of boiling water was added to raise it to a suitable temperature for washing grimy hands and faces. A new cake of Lava soap and fresh linen towels hung on the bottom rungs of the windmill awaited the first dusty, sweaty thresher.

The men slowly crossed the road, many of them smoking, all of them talking, enjoying their leisure as much as the prospect

of a meal. The splashes of water on their hands and faces invigorated them, and they laughed easily and loudly, their merriment
alerting the women of their presence. The farmwives swung into
action with the efficiency of a restaurant staff. One woman took
charge of the children to keep them from underfoot.

Another of the women worked to keep up with washing
dishes, as there were neither enough seats nor enough plates for
all twenty men to eat at the same time. The other two women
waited on table, bringing in fresh platters of chicken and refilling
the bowls of potatoes. My mother beamed as she watched the
men wolfing down her good cooking. She smiled at their praise
and laughed at their shy jokes.

Finally, the last of the men had eaten and joined the others
for a short rest on the lawn under the huge pine trees. Inevitably,
a few of them would start playing the game mumblety-peg, toss-
ing a jackknife into the air with both blades open, letting it fall
and stick in the grass. It was a contest of chance and skill, as each
possible landing was worth a number of points.

The women also ate and rested before they began a repeat
performance for the evening meal. This time it would be meatloaf,
potato salad, Jell-O with fruit, and cake.

Early in the evening the threshers would finish, and the next
morning, as the dew was drying on the oat shocks at the next farm
on Fred Pauls's circuit, that largest of machines on Pleasant Ridge
would begin its slow but inexorable rumble down the road. There,
another anxious housewife would have risen at dawn to start the
process all over again.

Getting Up Wood

Robert Frost wrote many words waxing poetic about the great outdoors, but the poem that sticks most in my mind is "Out, Out—," in which a boy loses a hand to an errant buzz saw, which

> Leaped out at the boy's hand, or seemed to leap—
> He must have given the hand. However it was,
> Neither refused the meeting. But the hand!
> The boy's first outcry was a rueful laugh,
> As he swung toward them holding up the hand
> Half in appeal, but half as if to keep
> The life from spilling.

I was a college student the first time I read these words, and they immediately brought to mind my father's accident.

On the day it happened, I arrived unknowingly from school, and as a responsible thirteen-year-old eighth grader, went out to the barn to begin the pre-milking chores even though my parents weren't home. I assembled the two milking machines and threw down silage and fed it with a topping of ground feed to the cows. At that point, Uncle Vern slid open the barn door on its track, stepped in, and then closed it behind him, interrupting my work. He stood under a light bulb, obviously disturbed, and I went over to him to find out what was wrong.

"Your dad had an accident in the woods," he said, and as I could see he was trying not to cry, my heart raced in fear. "But he's okay," my uncle assured me.

And then he explained. He and my father had been getting up wood, and as Paw was cutting a tree limb into stove lengths with the buzz saw, he slipped in the snow. As he tried to regain his balance, he inadvertently thrust his hand into the shrieking saw blade.

What Uncle Vern did not tell me was that he himself was so distraught by the accident that my father picked up his own severed finger. Holding his bleeding hand against his chest, he drove himself out of the woods and up to the house, pulling behind him the manure spreader that served as an all-purpose trailer on the farm. Back at the house, he stood while my mother wrapped his hand in a bath towel and then drove him the ten miles to the doctor's office in Richland Center, my father encouraging her all the way to drive faster, faster, faster.

The buzz saw had lopped off my father's right index finger and cut into the adjacent middle finger. Because the thick teeth of the saw had made a ragged cut, the finger could not have been reattached even if our small-town doctor had had the skill. But the middle finger was saved.

My uncle and I milked the cows that first night, but for the next several days, my mother and I handled the milking together, getting up early in the morning to complete the task in time for me to go to school, and milking again in the evening, finishing when it was almost my bedtime.

My father worried about the work he couldn't do, the pain pills not as effective as we had hoped, and when he went back to the doctor's office for a checkup, we learned that the stump of his finger was not healing properly. The physician had tried to save as much of the remaining finger as possible, but that portion ultimately required a second amputation, delaying my father's recovery.

My mother and I milked twice daily and managed the other chores as best we could, but I was a small thirteen-year-old; when I took my football physical for high school in the fall, I weighed 102 pounds. When I became ill from exhaustion, my father returned to chores even though his hand hadn't completely healed. He worked as best he could using only his left hand, his bandaged right hand protected by a plastic bread wrapper.

Paw's hand eventually did heal, although phantom pains continued for weeks. He frequently spilled cups of coffee when he picked up a mug, gripping the handle from habit only to remember the missing finger when coffee ran across the table top.

The stub of my father's missing finger resembled miniature buttocks. This helped to soften the alarm his grandchildren felt years later when they looked at his hand. When he laughed, so did they.

Getting up wood was a universal activity when I was growing up. Natural gas, propane, and fuel oil were not options, and coal was an expensive alternative. Every Driftless Area farm on the ridge had forested land too steep or rugged to be tilled, and trees not only could be sold for lumber, contributing to the economic diversity on farms, but also were a ready source of fuel. Tree limbs were a by-product of lumber sales, and fallen trees could not be sold for timber. Subsequently, a winter's fuel was in effect free for the taking if a farmer was willing to bring the muscle power to the task.

Some rural families worked up a season's firewood in the fall, stacking stove wood near the house to stoke the furnace or the parlor stove. We were not that kind of family, as our falls were taken up with picking corn, not only our own but for others as custom work. My father tended to work up enough wood to throw in a basement window and heat our house for a week or two, and after it was gone, he'd return to the woods for more.

As an adolescent, I would help get up wood on weekends,

loading stove wood in the spreader and dragging small branches to a burning pile.

Those of us who have been warmed by wood furnaces will insist that the heat is warmer than that from coal or fuel oil or natural gas. Standing next to a parlor stove or to the grill of a heat duct, home dwellers feel a warmth and security that will sustain them throughout the winter, even though they may scoff at the adage that a wood fire warms three times: from the effort of getting up the wood, from the satisfaction of a job well done, and, of course, from the heat of the burning wood.

But the free heat could come at a cost far dearer than that of purchasing coal. Inspired by the dual warnings of Frost and real life, I penned my own poem, titled "Buzz":

No one spoke when we made wood
because when the buzz saw talked everyone had to listen.
The eighteen-inch round saw blade turned by the tractor's
    power take-off
whined and screamed and moaned like a demented fishwife
    as we fed it tree limbs.
Someone watching from a far hill
would have seen a silent movie
the buzz saw dubbing for the piano
and would have thrilled at the drama
my father slipping in the snow
falling redly
his hand into the saw.

Down on the Farm, TV Style

On Pleasant Ridge we didn't purchase a television set until I was ten years old. And what a source of amusement it was for us to sit in that eerie blue glow and view a black-and-white world beyond the ridge. But occasionally we'd find the TV a funhouse mirror reflecting a rural life that we had never experienced and suspected had never existed. It became a game with us to see who could first identify TV-land's fantasies about country living.

One of the earliest mistaken notions of farm life that I remember occurred on *Lassie*. We all delighted in the program, but to our disgust, Lassie was continually licking her masters in the face, and those people not only tolerated these sloppy dog kisses but actually seemed to enjoy them. Even as children, we were very much aware of a farm dog's diet and personal hygiene. As much as we loved our farm dogs, we never exchanged kisses with them, nor did any other farm kids, as we knew all the nasty places that dog tongue had been.

On countless programs ranging from *Lassie* to *Gunsmoke*, Hollywood farmers amused us as they moved hay with pitchforks. A man who certainly looked like a farmer would reveal himself as a sham when he grasped the fork near the end of the handle and inexpertly worried little tufts of hay about with it. My paw, on the other hand, used a pitchfork as it was intended. With his left hand as a fulcrum, he'd hold the handle near the tines and then apply leverage with his right hand nearer the end of the handle. Rapidly, he'd pitch bunches of hay into a good-sized mound, and then he'd jab into it with the fork, staggering off with a fork-load of hay weighing almost as much as he did.

Now I've left the farm behind me, dogs and pitchforks included, but not the memories. And I still smile at the vision of rural life evoked by television producers. One year, I laughed as purported pioneers Samantha Eggar and Hal Holbrook chopped down trees to clear the land. They each grasped the middle of their ax handles and chipped away at their trees with the enthusiasm but hardly the efficiency of woodpeckers. I figure it would have taken them about a week to fell each tree. A real farmer-woodsman chokes up on the handle with his right hand, but then lets that hand slide back to join the other during the course of the swing, enabling him to add his weight along with his strength to the force of the blow as the ax flashes along its arc.

On one TV program, Jason Robards showed his city grandson how to milk cows by hand. In his demonstration, he pulled two teats simultaneously. In real life, the cow would have looked around, eyes wide and ears perked, as if to ask, "What the hell?"

Any dairy farmer knows that a good hand milker develops a rhythm by alternately squeezing and pulling with first one hand and then the other. To a listener in the barn, a continuous stream of frothing milk sings away in the pail, not dribbling patters followed by long pauses.

Perhaps the most incredible vision of farm family life appeared on an episode of *Little House on the Prairie*, a show that bore only a passing resemblance to its source material but provided endless amusement in its attempts to portray pioneer life. In one especially egregious example, the Ingalls family, living in the 1870s or '80s, decided to relax by going on a family camping trip!

Cheerfully, they "roughed it," enjoying the novelty of sleeping in tents, Pa fishing while Ma blissfully dragged her long skirts in the dirt preparing meals over a campfire.

Remember that in reality the Ingalls family would have spent years living in covered wagons and crude cabins with no plumbing or electricity. In actuality, they had been "camping" all of their pioneer lives by necessity. Recreational camping would have had only slightly less appeal for them than riding stationary exercise bicycles.

On another episode of *Little House*, Michael Landon busted one hundred acres of prairie sod in only three or four days' time. According to my own paw, old-timers claimed a man had to walk seven miles behind a horse-drawn plow to turn over one acre of land. Pa Ingalls's heroic feat of cultivation would have required him to walk seven hundred miles, making him the envy of Kenyan marathoners. Imagine, if you will, plodding along behind oxen as you plow your way from Madison to Little Rock, Arkansas—in less than four days—and then you can appreciate the absurdity of Farmer Landon's accomplishment.

The role of farmwife was also misrepresented on numerous occasions. On both *The Waltons* and *Family*, I've watched women-folk make pumpkin pie from scratch, using the huge watery ornamental variety, not the little ones raised for pies. I reckon you'd get about ten to twelve pies out of one large Halloween-style pumpkin, and not a one of them fit to eat. The pie prepared on *Family* was especially unusual; in a couple hours' time, a pumpkin almost the size of a bushel basket reappeared on the table as a pie. California chroniclers of the good rural life would be indeed amazed at the length of time required to cook pumpkin down to a proper pie consistency.

On the same *Family* episode, a supposedly modern California farmwife fed her chickens by casting the grain to her hens as they scurried about on the ground pecking up the kernels. My grandmother confirmed my suspicion that farmwives stopped feeding their chickens that way before the end of the nineteenth century. When I was a boy, grain was ground, nutrients artificially added, and the product fed from special chicken feeders to birds that many times never left the confines of the henhouse until their demise.

During the years of my young manhood, an increasing number of city folks sought the good life on a farm, attempting to pick up the tried-and-true old ways of doing things. Since many of those modern homesteaders may have learned about farm techniques from television, they probably encountered a number of unpleasant surprises when they actually found themselves down on the farm coping with dogs, pitchforks, axes, plows, pumpkins, hens, and most of all, former farmers like myself, smirking at their efforts.

Television, at least, has learned a few lessons since the airing of the original *Lassie*, *Little House on the Prairie*, and *The Waltons*. In addition to writers and filmmakers, producers often enlist the help of consultants to avoid anachronisms. But as small dairy farms have been replaced by mega-farms on the one hand and small specialty farms on the other—hobby, organic, dairy goat— fewer and fewer of us are left to fact-check their work.

Memorial Day on Pleasant Ridge

When I die, I reckon I'd as soon be buried on Pleasant Ridge as anywhere. There, a small cemetery flanks an empty tall-steepled white country church. From the kitchen window of the house where I was raised as a boy, we had a distant view of this bucolic setting.

In the older part of the graveyard, white crumbly headstones sit at angles under sleepy pines. Clumps of orange lilies, peonies, and lilacs dot the marker-studded lawn, with an occasional old garden rose scenting the air. Blackberry bushes, black-eyed Susans, and goldenrod stand sentinel along the fence rows that separate the cemetery from the adjoining fields.

My father and two others from the community acted as cemetery trustees, parceling out lots and overseeing the care of the graves. Under their supervision, grass was neatly mowed and trimmed, a part of the perpetual care provision included in the purchase of a cemetery plot.

Every Memorial Day, my mother sent me into the woods and meadows to find wildflowers. Depending on seasonal conditions, I picked wild geraniums and violets, ferns and mayflowers. Our lawn yielded tulips, lilacs, peonies, and mock orange blossoms.

We arranged bouquets in either glass mayonnaise jars that had been washed clean or in orange juice cans that had been de-lidded with a can opener and covered with aluminum foil.

On the car drive to the cemetery, we kids each balanced a

bouquet between our feet and held another in our hands. At the graveyard, we added water and then carefully positioned them at the headstones of our relatives, the Grays and the Johnsons, ancestors who had been laid to rest in the clay bosom of the ridge.

On the Sunday before Memorial Day, the church congregation honored the dead formally. All the children in the Sunday school lined up before the altar while the Sunday school superintendent, Sandy Mott, distributed the little flags the town had purchased for that purpose. Sunday school teacher Minnie Williams gave each child a nosegay of garden flowers that the ladies of the church had brought from home.

As Mae Buroker plunked the stirring chords of "Onward Christian Soldiers," we marched down the aisle, out the door into the sunshine, and filed into the cemetery. We searched out the little wrought iron star flag holders that denoted military veterans, stuck in the flags, and propped the bouquets against the gravestones. Ladies of the congregation, clutching lace-edged hankies, helped the smaller children.

We were unusually quiet as we worked at our task, sensing the solemnity of the occasion. The adults in the congregation watched in near silence. Some of the farmers cleared their throats while a number of women twisted their handkerchiefs. When the last flag and the final bouquet had been stationed at the remaining veteran's grave, old Reverend Lester Matthews offered up a prayer under the blue May sky while the ridge folk stood with bowed heads.

Many of those parishioners have since passed away and are now buried in the little Pleasant Ridge Cemetery themselves. And few people would use glass mayonnaise jars or foil-wrapped cans as improvised vases for flowers picked in the woods or cut from flowerbeds in their lawns. The church itself has been closed for years, but the pine trees remain, along with the clumps of orange lilies, peonies, lilacs, blackberry bushes, black-eyed Susans, and goldenrod.

~

Some folks consider cemeteries rather eerie places. As a child growing up on Pleasant Ridge, I soon got over that notion. I viewed the graveyard that flanked the little white Pleasant Ridge Evangelical United Brethren Church as just another part of my life. And even now, as I pot geraniums, I think back on that sleepy little cemetery.

When I was a preschooler, my mother began sending me to Vacation Bible School, which lasted one week every summer. The less vigilant teachers permitted us to play among the graves. In lieu of a playground, the headstones were wonderful climbing structures, or hiding places in games of hide-and-seek, or obstacles during games of tag.

Although some might consider this a lack of respect for the dead, I know I would prefer to have laughing children playing on the earth above me than a drooping spray of fading plastic flowers.

One summer, when I was a teenager, I earned spending money by helping mow the cemetery grass. It was cash well earned. The mowing was slow because I had to guide the mower close to the hundreds of headstones, temporarily remove grave markers, and move potted geraniums and plastic floral arrangements.

I soon learned that if a potted plant had even a hint of green left on it, or a plastic bouquet still bore a trace of color, some mourners expected it to remain a loving tribute on the grave.

After all these years, I still can summon up the sensory impressions connected with mowing that country cemetery. I can smell the freshly cut grass, the warm petroleum scent of the power mower, and the lushness of the wild berry bushes along the fence row. I can see the verdant leaves of the orange lilies crowding the base of an old gnarled lilac bush.

After completing the task, with aching muscles I would survey the newly mown cemetery, and the sight never failed to give me a satisfied feeling. I had transformed the overgrown field into a manicured park.

One memory of the cemetery brings a smile—the great outhouse flap. The outdoor toilet behind the church had decayed to the point where it, too, should have been buried. A member of the congregation who had carpentry skills built a large new outdoor privy with separate adjacent compartments for men and women. The new building was placed halfway down the hill of the gravel parking lot between the road and the cemetery.

A controversy ensued. One of the largest clans on the ridge had a huge plot at the roadside edge of the graveyard. As it was a source of pride to the family, they lavishly adorned it each Memorial Day.

Unfortunately, the new privy obstructed the view of the plot from the road. The young toilet builder was so upset with the criticism directed at his act of charity that in the middle of the night, he whisked the toilet off the grounds and hid it in his woods.

For several days, ridge folk scratched their heads, puzzling over the mystery of the disappearing toilet, suspecting an outhouse caper and keeping their eyes open hoping to discover it annexed behind some neighbor's house. Finally, the conscience-stricken carpenter returned it, and, as a compromise, relocated the building to the foot of the hill, allowing passersby a panoramic view of the centerpiece cemetery lot.

~

When the first frost is on the horizon and my geraniums continue to bloom on my patio, I remember the Pleasant Ridge EUB Cemetery, now the resting place of my parents as well as other ancestors.

And I remember my younger brother standing at the foot of the stairs, his arms outstretched to bar my way as I carried pots of geraniums to winter in the room we shared. He did not appreciate my enthusiasm for them, but as the bigger sibling, I prevailed.

I had developed an early interest in plants, but as I lacked the cash to buy them, I learned propagation techniques. Geraniums were easy; one clipping placed in a glass of water soon developed roots and was ready for a pot of dirt, and if put outside during the summer, quickly became a magnificent, lavishly blooming plant.

And now comes the moment of full disclosure, as the statute of limitations has long passed.

When I was young, people often honored their departed relatives and friends by placing potted geraniums beside grave markers on Memorial Day. I would wait until a few weeks had passed, and then bicycle over to the cemetery, plastic bread wrappers stuffed in a back pocket. Discreetly, with the practiced care of a master gardener, I would take inconspicuous geranium cuttings, adding to the colors in my collection, and then pedal quickly home to root them in water. By summer's end, I had every possible shade of red, pink, and white available in the world of geraniums.

Now, rather than resorting to grave robbing, I purchase small rooted geraniums from a big-box discount store, repot them, and with generous doses of water and fertilizer, quickly bring them to an impressive size resplendent with blooms.

Yes, I reckon I'd as soon be buried on Pleasant Ridge as anywhere. The time has passed when I could have sat down with the cemetery trustees, studied the creased and penciled map of grave plots over a cup of coffee, and for twenty-five dollars purchased a grassy spot under a nodding pine, a real bargain for eternal peace.

But I might still have my ashes scattered in the breeze over the graves of my ancestors, ashes to ashes, dust to dust, resting eternally on the clay bosom of the ridge.

I remember the days when the cemetery was as alive and vital as the church sitting beside it. Now Memorial Day is celebrated with an open house at the restored but empty church, when people return and remember, some of them, no doubt, finding a place to tuck a potted geranium.

When Angels Wore Bedsheets

On the afternoon of the Christmas program, Guy Williams would walk across the road from his farm to the Pleasant Ridge EUB Church to stoke up the furnace, an antiquated heating system that did little more than take the chill out of the drafty old building. Down the road at our farm, we started chores early, and I didn't dawdle putting the milking machines together.

The church was half full by the time my family arrived, as Christmas and Easter were the two occasions when nearly everyone on the ridge attended. Going to a service at night was a novelty. On Sunday mornings, the huge room was inviting, filled with light from the tall, clear-paned windows. But at night the shadows transformed the familiar setting into one both intimate and remote, depending on whether I glanced at the faces crowded together in the dark oak pews or at the blank windows.

The sight of Gramp and Granny already seated in the congregation—him wearing his teeth for the occasion and her fidgeting with a Christmas corsage—banished all thoughts of remoteness.

The scent of cologne mingled with the earthier smells of the barn on those of us who had just finished milking and with the woodsy smell of pine from the Christmas tree. A wispy white pine from Sandy Mott's woods was positioned up front to the left. It was decorated with a miscellany of Christmas ornaments, some handmade with more love than craft, such as the shiny snowflakes snipped from tin coffee can lids with tin shears.

Along the front of the church, faded brown curtains hung on a wire stretched from one side of the church to the other for the occasion. Behind it, the picture of Jesus remained, but the old Victorian parlor table that served as an improvised altar had been temporarily moved down to the basement to make more room on the stage.

After a good-bye glance at my folks, my sister and I joined the other children who were taking their places behind the curtains, shushing one another to silence. My toddler brother Larry had to stay behind. My mother tried to entertain him while chatting with her good friend Dorothy Johnson.

Mae Buroker, with her wreath of graying red braids haloing her squinting smile, shed her coat and took her place on the piano bench. After flexing her arthritic fingers for a moment, she flipped to the Christmas carol section of the hymnal and began thumping her way through those familiar tunes while the remainder of the audience filed into the church.

Finally, the moment arrived. Someone flicked the light switch and the church dimmed, illuminated only by the tree and the lamps doubling as stage lights. The audience hushed in anticipation as the rings hissed along the wire, the curtains opening on Margaret Ann, my little sister.

With freshly washed blond hair and a red taffeta dress that my mother had made for the occasion, she was a vision of childhood beauty. Saucily swinging her arms and grinning impishly, she chirped through a poem of welcome.

Many of the recitations had been performed a week earlier at the grade school Christmas program and tended to celebrate the coming of Santa Claus rather than the birth of Christ, such as cousin Don's recitation of "'Twas the Night Before Christmas." Others had been practiced in the church on preceding Sunday afternoons. My poem retelling the glory of Christ's birth was of that sort. My head buzzed and my palms perspired as I concentrated on a perfect rote delivery, staring at my freshly polished shoes.

Mae slid back from the piano to make room for my Uncle Vern, an angular farmer-pianist with weather-reddened cheeks and work-callused fingers. Those hands that milked cows and shoveled manure could perform an impressive chord-rippling version of "Star of the East."

The minister's granddaughter, ten-year-old Nancy, her glasses magnifying her eyes and her white knee socks at half-mast, diligently wheezed her halting progress through an accordion solo of "Whispering Hope."

Balding bachelor John Merriott in a vintage tan houndstooth sports coat faced the piano rather than the audience, hands behind his back, and bellowed a basso rendition of "O Holy Night." As this was an annual performance, we children had all perfected imitations of old John's vibrato style, and while some of us backstage sang along sotto voce, the rest of us stifled giggles and poked one another.

The highlight of the evening was the pageant: angels in bedsheets and gold tinsel halos, shepherds in bathrobes with canes, and wise men in kimonos that were Ben Denman's souvenirs of World War II.

Betty MacDonald, cloaked in a blue-dyed sheet, portrayed Mary. A pretty girl, she was especially radiant that night, and no one could tell that the skirt she wore under it was hemmed with safety pins, as she had run out of time making it. The words of the Christmas story, as familiar as a mother's face, never lost their impact, even if the reader, with more spirit than skill, informed us that "Mary was with great child."

At the conclusion of the pageant, Reverend Matthews clambered on the stage in his baggy serge suit, and after loudly clearing his throat and beaming smiles in all directions, offered the benediction.

The tolling of the church bell announced the arrival of Santa Claus, who in his red and white flannel suit and matted-cotton beard bore a striking resemblance to Gordon MacDonald, a co-incidence we all chose to ignore. He distributed small paper bags filled with hard candy, peanuts in the shell, and apples. Children gave their Sunday school teachers gifts—my mother had bought a lace-trimmed hanky for me to give to Minnie Williams—and in return received a memento, sometimes a Bible bookmark.

After gifts had been opened, treats sampled, and performances complimented, we returned home, the community Christmas observance in the Pleasant Ridge EUB Church a prelude to our family celebrations that were reserved for the actual holiday. We'd drive to Richland Center on Christmas Eve to look at the pretty decorations on the fashionable side of town that we of more modest means denigrated as "Mortgage Hill," but just as we were about to leave, Mother would worry she had left the iron plugged in and go back inside the house for a few minutes. Off we'd drive, scraping frost from windows in preparation for viewing strings of colored lights, and then we'd return home to find that Santa had visited during our absence.

After the doors were closed in the EUB church, gradually the fire in the basement furnace would die. The sanctuary, illuminated only by starlight, would cool and wait patiently for the coming Sunday morning service.

Minnie and Mae

The names Minnie and Mae were conversationally linked in our Pleasant Ridge neighborhood, like Tom and Jerry, Amos and Andy, Mutt and Jeff. Both enjoyed recreational rubbering on the telephone party line—secretly listening to private telephone conversations on party lines, commonly shared by up to ten households in rural areas in the 1940s and '50s.

And both Minnie and May were church ladies, Minnie teaching Sunday school and Mae playing the piano for Sunday services. Minnie sometimes picked flowers from her garden and arranged them in a tall-handled white wicker basket to place in front of the altar. And physically they were a matched set as well, like a pair of salt and pepper shakers, both short and heavy, their hair braided and then pinned in crowns. While Minnie lived across the road from the Pleasant Ridge Evangelical United Brethren Church, Mae lived in the house next to the church. The women were anchors during services, with Mae seated near the piano and Minnie by a back window on the east side. Although married, they both sat alone, as neither husband set foot in the sanctuary except to lend manpower for banquets in the basement.

Because the church lacked a well, these banquets required milk cans of water to be brought in. Minnie's husband Guy might bring one, and Mae's husband Elmer, on occasion, the second, carrying them down the cement steps, grunting and straining at the weight (both were skinny farm men resisting retirement, who still wore the same size overalls they had when young and muscular, before hard work had begun to sap muscle size rather than build it). After depositing their cans at the spot on the kitchen floor where the ladies all pointed, then briefly touching their engineer-style striped hats, they quickly made their retreat up the steps as ladies called, "Thanks!" in their wake.

I never saw much of Elmer, usually only glimpses of him. When my siblings and I knocked on Mae's door for Halloween trick-or-treating, she answered with laughing and clapping, delighted at the cleverness of our costumes. Basking in her praise, we helped ourselves to modest selections from her candy bowl, and then, laughing still more, she would urge us to take more and more. We could hear broadcast voices and smell tobacco, indicating that Elmer was listening to the radio and smoking his pipe in the rose-papered parlor where Mae's upright piano sat, but she never called him to come see us. Apparently, children for him were like churches, best enjoyed from a distance.

Minnie's husband Guy seemed similarly scarce. Once an exemplary student, Minnie had taken an achievement examination upon her high school graduation to determine if she had acquired the necessary knowledge to become a grade school teacher. After passing the test, she found herself the next fall in a one-room school in front of a couple dozen students ranging in age from five to fourteen. Soon after, she met a young farmer who lived in her school district and agreed to marry him, resigning her teaching position. She moved into the farmhouse Guy's parents had owned. And just as she had begun teaching when little more than a girl, now she began married life, preparing meals in the kitchen with cupboards and woodwork painted a pale green and giving birth to babies in a floral-papered bedroom. When her children left the nest, she returned to teaching, this time at Sunday school, with a half dozen children at most and only for an hour each week.

Guy had been a good husband, but like many couples, they spent long hours apart. He was out in the barn milking cows or in the field tending to crops, while she maintained their home. When she went to church Sunday morning, he smoked his pipe and read the newspaper in their living room. Their lives intersected in the kitchen and in the bedroom.

During her summers, Minnie filled her front porch with rows of potted house plants, some in wicker stands. She especially took pride in her jade plant, a huge succulent in a giant clay pot. It had grown so large that each spring when Guy moved it out onto the porch, he told her that he might not be man enough to move it back inside come winter.

When I was a teenager, Minnie took a slip for me from her jade plant. After letting it grow roots in a glass of water, I potted it. As years passed, my jade plant grew larger and larger until eventually it was good sized, but never as large as Minnie's plant loomed in my memory.

As she aged, Mae moved more and more slowly, her legs encased in brown cotton stockings, her feet shod in thick-heeled shoes, as she worked her way up the aisle of the Pleasant Ridge EUB Church to her piano. There she took her seat, ready to accompany hymn singing. She remained seated until Reverend Lester Matthews began his sermon, at which point she rose carefully from the creaking piano bench and resettled herself on the short pew next to the piano.

Mae seemed to sense when Lester was winding down. Moving with the stealth of a housebreaker, she hoisted herself to a crouching position and steadied herself with a grip on the piano, returned to her bench, her hands poised for the final hymn of the service.

My Uncle Vern played piano, the only ridge farmer to do so,

at least the only one who had stayed with lessons long enough to acquire the degree of skill and confidence to play for an audience. He was always asked to play a solo for the church Christmas program. Although Mae joined in the praise of my uncle's performance, I have wondered if she might have felt jealous or overlooked. I had heard grownups tell one another in quiet voices that she didn't always play all of the notes, that she sometimes improvised her own chords in the left hand rather than playing the song as written. Other than those faint criticisms, no one seemed to pay any more notice to her weekly efforts than if she had been the furnace in the church basement.

Sometimes the Youth Fellowship sang for the Sunday service on special occasions. Usually, Mae came to the church to play for our practice, but once when our youth directors Sandy and Cody couldn't make it, we gathered at her house for practice, all of us clustered around the piano in the tiny flower-papered room.

After all of us agreed that our rendition of "Bringing in the Sheaves" was as good as it was going to get, Mae began playing rollicking tunes on her piano—to our amazement, as in our innocence, we felt that her old upright only worked with hymns. Then she called to Elmer, who opened a door and emerged reluctantly from their bedroom. "Get your spoons," she directed, her face ruddier than the fading sunset of her graying hair, and to our surprise, he hurried to the kitchen and returned with two tablespoons. He sat on a straight-backed chair in the crowded parlor, and as Mae played, he held the spoons in one hand, one spoon on top of the other, in such a manner that when he tapped them against his thigh, they made the ringing sound of castanets. Mae played faster and faster as Elmer played along with her, the spoons dancing up and down and around his skinny legs as if they had a life of their own, and some of the girls in our group spontaneously began to do an improvised dance.

When Mae stopped playing and turned to us, we expected a scolding about the impropriety of dancing (one of the thou-shalt-nots in EUB church doctrine), but instead she said in a conspiratorial whisper, "I don't think it would matter if you danced. Just push the furniture back against the walls." She began playing again, Elmer providing accompanying percussion, and we slid back tables and chairs and floor lamps to make an open space in the center of the room, dancing like angels on the head of a pin, careening into one another as we joyously flailed about in time to the music.

At last, when it was time to go home, Mae became very solemn. "Don't tell Sandy and Cody," she cautioned, and we silently nodded in agreement.

When I was a boy, clergymen were always men. Samuel Johnson once said of women preachers that it "was like a dog walking on its hind legs. It is not well done but you are surprised to find it done at all." Few people on the ridge had heard of Johnson, but they would have agreed with him.

Shoving this misogynous attitude aside, in retrospect, church ladies helped keep the institution afloat. Minnie and Mae might have been gossips, their appearance easily caricatured, but in reality, they were both talented ladies, and I remember them not for their religious devotion but as pillars of the community, women who were relegated by the times to roles as powers behind the throne. Their humanity softened our lives on the ridge.

The Church Band

The Pleasant Ridge EUB Church band did not have seventy-six trombones to lead a big parade, nor did we have a hundred and ten cornets close at hand. But we had our very own music man in Reverend Lester Matthews.

The reverend's day job was clerking in a hardware store in town, work that no doubt supported his Sunday calling, officiating at two services, first at the Pleasant Ridge EUB Church and then down the valley to the Buck Creek Church for a second. He might have had little interest in starting up a band if it hadn't been for me, an aspiring young musician limited both by a modest talent and a mother who could not bear to hear me practice, shouting at me to take my Flutophone outside if I wanted to play it. But what I lacked in musicianship I made up for in versatility. In addition to the plastic wannabe recorder, I played piano (self-taught, sneaking over to the church on my bike to practice on the EUB upright), flute (the high school band director talked me into it at the end of my sophomore year), and clarinet (the fingering was similar to a flute).

I belonged to the EUB Youth Fellowship, as did every other non-Catholic farm kid eager for a social life on the ridge, and when someone told me that Reverend Matthews had a complete set of sheet music for marching band from an earlier youthful enterprise, I approached him with my idea for forming a church band and learned that he had not only the music but music stands and even a snare drum.

He scratched his chin thoughtfully as I explained that because nearly everyone in the Youth Fellowship was in band at Ithaca High School, we had enough musicians to cover all the parts. To clinch the deal, I told him we would need him to be our conductor.

And so the Pleasant Ridge Evangelical United Brethren Church Band was formed, a roster of musicians not much lengthier than the name of our group. At our first rehearsal, about a dozen musicians showed up and covered most of the parts, although some of us had to share music stands. Our sound was good and loud, perhaps the acoustical effect of the cement block walls and the low ceiling of the church basement where we were practicing. Although we were fewer in number, we sounded almost as good as the high school band, and some of the marches we played were the same ones we had performed in school.

Our preacher-turned-band director waved his arms while we played, more keeping time with us than setting a tempo or suggesting dynamics, but he was doing his best, his red face beaded with perspiration on his forehead.

In retrospect, I realize that our ensemble was more like a wind chamber group, with generally only one instrument to a part. In addition to our adult trombone and trumpet players, musicians included cousin Kay on bass clarinet, my sister on flute, cousin Don on drums, neighbor girl Sharon on first clarinet, me on second, and Sharon's brother Junior on baritone horn. Alan Subera, who was only a freshman but the best musician in the high school band, played tuba. My uncle Vern was the only trombonist, and one trumpeter whose name I have long since forgotten drove up from Richland Center for practice in our church basement.

We had only two gigs, our first a talent show that was performed one warm summer night on a hay wagon pulled under a yard light next to the front steps of the church as an improvised stage. We would have had more room on the raised platform at the front of the church, but out of deference to the sensibilities of the more devout churchgoers, I thought it best that we played "Washington Post" and the rest of our limited march repertoire out in the open air. Our audience was a small but very appreciative crowd that enjoyed the novelty of a church band.

Our second concert was held as a part of the christening of the new pole shed that the father of Don and Kay Johnson had completed earlier that summer. The structure served as our concert hall, and once again, a hay wagon served as our stage. This time, Don and Kay's little sister Judy sat under it providing Lawrence Welk–style soap bubbles. Our audience applauded dutifully, but while we had gotten better as a group, we were less of a novelty.

And the summer was coming to an end. I was going back to college in the fall and the other student musicians, back to high school. Uncle Vern put his trombone back in the closet, and Reverend Matthews returned his sheet music, stands, and drum to the basement, and with them the memory of the one summer that the hills of Pleasant Ridge came alive with the sound of big band music.

The Catholics

For the evangelical folk on the ridge, our faith was conventional and our commitment casual. The Catholics, however, with their faithful adherence to elaborate rituals, seemed as exotic as if they had been Hasidic Jews.

As evangelicals, we went to church for the Christmas program several days prior to the holy day so that we could celebrate the actual holiday at home with Santa and our families. We kids recited poems, sang songs, and acted out the birth of Christ, the guys wearing bathrobes and the girls sheets, the closest we could come to Middle Eastern costumes.

We did go to church on Easter Sunday, as our religious observances did not interfere with the visit of the Easter Bunny. My mother made new dresses for the occasion, both for my sister and herself, and would put the ham in the oven before we drove to the steepled white frame church that I could see from my bedroom window.

The third regular attendance at church was Children's Day, the Sunday at the conclusion of a week of Vacation Bible School when our program was part of the worship service. While Mae sat at the upright piano, graying-red braids crowning her head, plunking out "Onward, Christian Soldiers," we marched in two lines. The two tallest kids led the way, one carrying the American flag, the other, the white Christian flag with its red cross. The lines diverged at the two aisles and rejoined on stage, standing in formation as the flags were repositioned in their holders. We sang hymns (always "Jesus Loves the Little Children") and recited Bible verses ("Suffer the little children to come unto me" was a favorite, although the suffering part was unsettling).

And then we were good, for the most part, until Christmas. True, we had those on the ridge who were regular in attendance, such as Minnie, who lived directly across the road from the church and taught a Sunday school class, Mae the pianist, and Sandy, who always came early Sunday morning during winter to fire up the wood furnace.

But otherwise, the congregation seemed to consist of a few stragglers, usually a total assembly of less than a dozen. Luckily Reverend Matthews had a day job clerking at a hardware store in town and a second EUB service down the valley at Buck Creek following ours.

In retrospect, the peripatetic personality of our pastor seemed fitting for the rather disengaged flock he shepherded on Pleasant Ridge, most of whom never took him literally. We were forbidden by church doctrine to dance, to play cards, to drink alcohol, and to attend the cinema, among other sins, but most of us winked at each other as we continued to transgress.

However, our Catholic neighbors marched to the more insistent beat of their own drummer. Their parish priest made pronouncements, and parishioners fell in line, especially regarding church attendance. Just as postal carriers pledge that "neither snow nor rain nor sleet nor hail nor gloom of night shall stay these couriers from the swift completion of their appointed rounds," our Catholic friends never let the natural elements keep them home on a Sunday morning. A heavy snow would find the entire family shoveling their long driveway, hoping the township snowplow would make it through in time for them to complete the ten-mile drive into town for Mass. We EUBs would have looked out our windows and respected the blizzard as God's will, even though some of us were within walking distance of our church.

Those of us who had been invited to Catholic weddings and had sat through a High Mass were impressed and confused by the devotion on display. No one understood a word of the Latin being spoken, and we were never certain when we should be standing, sitting, or kneeling. Despite the pageantry of the service, the colorful rituals, the comings and goings of the celebrants and participants, the Mass seemed very long.

Confession was another oddity, going into a telephone booth–like box and telling a priest, usually one you had known for years, about your private sins! The idea seemed rather embarrassing to us. We imagined that if we had to tell Reverend Matthews about our wrongdoings, he might gossip about them with neighbors who came into the hardware store.

The statues of the Virgin Mary that decorated lawns and the use of rosaries for prayer seemed exotic and magical. We had nothing like that in our religion, only pictures of Jesus, sometimes standing in a flock of sheep, with a mournful, worried look on his face.

Card-playing was a universal recreation on the ridge. Typically, a couple or two would be invited to play cards for the evening (often euchre, sometimes 500), drink beer, and end the evening with a lunch. A small child or two might be brought along and put to sleep atop the bed holding coats.

When our Catholic neighbors were either hosts or guests on a Friday night, lunch was never served before 12:01 so that the salami or big bologna could be brought out for sandwiches.

The Catholics seemed to belong to an exclusive club, one that appeared obsessive from the perspective of those of us who were lukewarm Protestants, and that lack of commitment no doubt contributed to the decline of our church.

The old Evangelical United Brethren church, after a merger

with the Methodist congregation, closed for many years. But now it has been restored, an artifact commemorating the Lord's Acre Sales, the Mother-Daughter and Father-Son banquets, the charity quilts pieced by the Ladies' Aid Society, and those programs at Easter and Christmas, when the church served as a spiritual center of the community. The gleaming white building with its impressive steeple looks as if it is waiting patiently for a new congregation to settle into its rows of vintage pews.

Now when I step inside the sanctuary, its hollow emptiness seems to flutter with the better angels of the long-ago community on the ridge during my boyhood.

Hills and Valleys

While it is true that we had a wonderful panoramic view from Pleasant Ridge and that on a clear day we almost could see forever, sometimes we nearly needed to put rocks in our pockets if we hoped to walk in a straight line from the house across the road to the barn.

If we were nestled in a valley, we would have been sheltered from the gale-force winds powering the windmill that pumped water from the ground when my great-grandfather lived on the farm. We could still see the basket-like crotches at the tops of the white pines in our lawn, the consequence of the trees being topped when they were younger so as not to obstruct the predominately western wind.

And if my great-grandpa had lived in the valley, rather than on the exposed spine of the ridge, we wouldn't need to pump water because it would have bubbled placidly out of the ground in springs, pure and cold.

From the top of the tower ladder in every direction that we turned, we could see faraway farms perched on the series of hills that made up the ridge. If we climbed the ladder on the exterior of the silo, or inside the barn up to the windows of the haymow, the effect was much like peering from a low-flying airplane.

But as a boy, I dismissed the view, even with a nighttime sky, the yard lights of distant farms twinkling like fallen stars, and the clustered lights of faraway Bunker Hill, like an earth-bound constellation.

My problem? The only water I saw was pumped from the ground, collected in the small milk house tank that cooled our cans of milk or in the stock tank that watered our cattle during the summer. The one exception was the spring snowmelt when the ravine in our woods temporarily became a river and I could trudge through slushy snow down the hill to marvel at the phenomenon, lamenting its ephemeral existence. Soon, my bank-threatening river would once again become a barren ditch, and my fantasies of fishing and boating and swimming would all be washed away.

On the other hand, my Johnson cousins, Don, Kay, and Judy, lived on the upper Little Willow Valley, a farmstead that in my mind could have been the setting for Rebecca's Sunnybrook Farm. The house was nestled at the head of a valley shaded by a giant cottonwood tree that snowed its down on the lawn in summer, a beautiful effect.

Behind their house, five springs merged like fingers of a hand into a brook that ran by the house, a constant lullaby during warm summer evenings when windows were open while the family slept. In the kitchen, a handpump brought cold water up from the springs. The stream continued down to the barn, where it ran through the milk house cooling the cans of fresh Jersey milk until the truck arrived and hauled them to the cheese factory.

But the centerpiece of the homestead was the house, now captured in pastels by family matriarch and outsider artist Naomi Johnson. The traditional farmhouse was well porched, with not only a screened porch facing the road but also one in back that opened onto the springs, and most wonderful of all, a double-decker on the end of the house facing the cottonwood tree and the bluff behind it. The lower level was open, with stairs leading to the screened top level, used by the Johnson grandparents, who lived in a second-story apartment.

The large dining room served as an open-concept family room, a term that didn't exist when I was a kid. A big parlor woodstove made the room cozy for dining at the large square table or for relaxing on the studio couch or rocking chair. But we all knew that the oversized easy chair with the brown leather upholstery cracked from wear and age was off limits to anyone but Verne Johnson himself, my first cousin once removed.

The family no longer owns that property, and the new owners have razed the kitchen–dining room wing of the house and remodeled the remaining two-story part into a modernized vacation rental home. They have landscaped the lawn and springs with native plants, all with the best of intentions for being environmentally responsible.

But for me, the charm is gone.

Maybe grass just seems greener in the valley to a child who was raised on hills.

Snowbound

Henry David Thoreau once proclaimed, "We do not ride on the railroad; it rides upon us," asserting that progress is sometimes an illusion, that for every one of mankind's steps forward, another step is taken back. No doubt he'd shake his head at the improvements in road and utility high-line maintenance if he traveled to Pleasant Ridge. Roadsides have been cleared of brush and trees and the banks graded flat. With these improvements, not only can farmers work their fields almost to the shoulders of the highways, but even more important, the roads themselves are less likely to be covered with snowdrifts, and tree limbs will no longer fall across power lines.

Maybe Thoreau would remember the hickories that grew along the road both to the east and to the west of our farm buildings on the ridge, some of them producing huge nuts free for our gathering. Perhaps he'd recall the wild blackberries, asparagus, mushrooms, and wildflowers that once grew there.

But people on the ridge no longer have to worry about being snowbound, as we were in the winter of 1958–59 when we received record snowfalls with high winds. The year before, when I was an eighth grader, my reading class had been led line by line over a period of weeks, it seemed, through John Greenleaf Whittier's famous poem *Snow-Bound*. The following year, we were living it.

Early in the winter, the snowplows had no problem keeping up, and the piles of snow mounded atop the natural banks of the road were impressive. But as the storms kept coming, the banks grew even higher, until at the top of the hill between the farm buildings of Ed Jansen and Otto Fry, the plows could no longer break their way through.

The truck that picked up our milk couldn't navigate the snow, and my father, faced with the dilemma of full cans and no milk pick up, could either start dumping milk or try to take it to the cheese factory himself. He loaded the full cans of milk onto the bed of his empty manure spreader (those were the days when milk inspection was a far more casual activity), threw a scoop shovel in with them, and headed down County D, hoping to make it through the two miles of snowdrifts to Highway 80, which as a major thoroughfare would certainly be plowed.

At Barney Mick's farm, he stopped to enlist Barney's assistance and haul his milk as well, and off they went, down the Mick Hill, past the Rose's flats, around the corner of Buck Creek School toward the intersection of 80 by the Buck Creek gas station.

This latest snowstorm was technically a blizzard, but Ithaca High School, where I was enrolled as a freshman, had been late calling in the buses to take us home. Although the lumbering yellow vehicles could muscle their way through the deep snow in the valley, the ridge was another matter. The driver let me off at the Johnson farm, the last stop in upper Little Willow before ascending the hill to Pleasant Ridge. Verne was my father's first cousin, Dorothy was my mother's best friend, and she immediately called to let Ma know that I was safe and would stay at the Johnsons until the roads were cleared.

Becoming snowbound in a blizzard today is serious business, as the storms are usually accompanied by a power outage that means no source of heat, and even if a family has stockpiles of food, they have no way to cook it. When Ralph Waldo Emerson speaks of self-reliance, many modern folks don't fully grasp what he's talking about.

But being stranded at the Johnson farm was like looking at the illustrations of Whittier's famous poem. A handpump in the kitchen provided fresh water from the spring that flowed past the outhouse down to the milk house to cool the milk and serve as another refrigerator during the summer. Because the large dining room was heated by a big square woodburning space heater, in winter it doubled as a family room.

In the fall, Verne Johnson shot and cleaned squirrels that Dorothy chicken-fried. In the spring, maple sap in a cake pan atop the woodstove evaporated to maple sugar. In the summer, the men folk would take a bar of soap and towels for bathing in the creek.

While I was snowbound, I hoped that the snow would never melt.

Dorothy had an old manual typewriter that fascinated me. Next year, as a sophomore, I planned to take typing, because I hoped to be a writer. And although I had no understanding of the touch method, I thought I could get a head start by hunting and pecking.

Because school was canceled and the snow was too deep to play outside, my cousin Don and I reached the point where we entertained ourselves by roughhousing. Dorothy eventually lost her patience. She stood with her hands at her waist peering over the top of her glasses at me. "I think it's about time for you to go home," she said, and I felt chastened.

The next day, the plows managed to finish clearing all the places where the roads on the ridge had been drifted shut, and I returned to my ordinary life at home.

Henry David Thoreau maintained that technological advances sometimes make our lives more complicated, not better. As I look across the ridge now where fence rows have for the most part gone away, I nod in agreement. The number of small farmers has dwindled, giving way to large corporate operations. Cattle are generally kept in feedlots rather than in pastures, and subsequently, good neighbors have nothing to do with good fences.

"We don't have neighbors anymore," one housewife whose farmer husband now owns a thousand acres lamented. "I seldom see anyone!"

Students nowadays are rarely asked to read *Snow-Bound*, and if they do, the life described in the poem seems as remote and exotic to them as does that in *The Arabian Nights*.

Mixed Nuts

My farmer parents were not convinced that I really needed the engineer boots I so desperately wanted when I was in eighth grade. They couldn't understand that a ninety-pound boy who was five feet tall required something to jump start his manhood, a little instant height and kick-ass attitude, a little *On the Road*, even if it was gravel in rural Willow Township.

With the resourcefulness that came down to me by way of generations of subsistence farmers, I took matters into my own hands. That fall, I picked up hickory nuts, nearly every day after school and on weekend afternoons, in all kinds of weather. (Well, sometimes when it was drizzling a bit.) I had my mother place an ad for me in the *Richland Center Shopping News*. "Hickory nuts for sale," it read, along with our phone number.

I laid newspapers over the linoleum on the floor of my room and spread my growing inventory of hickory nuts to dry, waiting for the phone to ring. And it did. My mother took orders, and when my folks drove into town on Saturdays to buy groceries and grind grist at the feed mill, they took me along to deliver hickory nuts.

When I had saved enough to buy the engineer boots, they fit perfectly, and while I still wasn't the tallest kid in the school, I felt the biggest. Ours was a hardscrabble farm, and rather than selfishly begging my parents to change their minds, I had been self-reliant and could wear my boots proudly.

My decision to pick up hickory nuts as a moneymaker emerged logically from the hickory nut culture around me. Hickories flourished in the pastures of our farm and on the banks along the road by our house. And my family had picked up hickory nuts for generations.

Gathering hickory nuts, like hunting morel mushrooms and picking wild blackberries, established our identity as a people, separating us from the Chicago city slicker who moved his family to the farm up the road to the east of us. He bragged to us that he had pecan trees growing in his woods and that he and his family had picked up a wagonload that he would sell for a small fortune.

We gently explained he had picked up bitternuts that, unfortunately, were inedible, not pecans, which grew only in the South. Bitternut trees look like smooth-bark hickories, and the nuts, like smooth hickory nuts. I grew up immediately knowing the difference between those varieties of nuts, just as at a glance I could distinguish between a cow and a bull.

My mother had a special stone for cracking hickory nuts, one that had been handed down through the family. It was round, about the diameter of a saucer and the fatness of a thick book, a dull black in color, with an indentation in the center for cradling the nut. I asked my father about the provenance of the stone. He didn't know, just that his mother had had it as long as he could remember. My mother had a ball-peen hammer dedicated to the task.

My father would sometimes crack nuts for my mother, but she would pick the nuts out of their shells, an excellent job for a fidgety person who liked to have something to do while sitting. When I was a teenager, I'd pick nuts out for her while I watched television, motivated by the thought of eating the pecan pies she would make substituting hickory nuts; the chocolate chip cookies with, naturally, hickory nuts; the chocolate layer cakes topped with chopped hickory nuts; and the fudge and the brownies—all with hickory nuts.

For Thanksgiving, my wife, Lu, and I often make a hickory nut pie in memory of my mother and black walnut bread in memory of my mother-in-law.

She grew up a black walnut girl, not far from Belmont, the site of Wisconsin's first territorial capital. Her mother, too, cracked nuts, but following a different family tradition. My mother-in-law used a standard claw hammer to smash her black walnuts on a slotted iron weight from an old platform farm scale. My wife remembers pieces of the shells whizzing around the kitchen like shrapnel. The cookies and cakes, nut breads, and bars of her childhood were enhanced with the pungent flavor of those walnuts gathered on the family farm. She would say the nuts have more character than mild-tasting hickories.

Lu and I met in college, and although we had grown up only seventy-five miles from each other, we learned that our respective nut cultures were different, and the nuts became emblems of our blended families. I enjoy black walnuts, as I loved my mother-in-law, but I knew that she could never replace my own mother or the hickory nuts she used when she baked. And my wife, not surprisingly, felt the same way about my mother and the black walnuts that were an integral part of her own mother's baking.

While my mother never baked with black walnuts, and my wife's never used hickory nuts, our own family now uses both, but with the sense of passing time. Lu's childhood farm has new owners; likewise, the hickory pasture land on my boyhood farm has been sold, and the nut trees along the road have long since been cut in the interest of power lines and snow removal.

While pecans and English walnuts are readily available in grocery stores, hickory nuts and black walnuts must be purchased online for prices akin to French truffles. Thankfully, a few years ago we purchased a second home in Platteville to spend winters. To our delight, we have a mature black walnut tree in our back lawn and hickory nut trees bordering a university parking lot across the street from us.

Our childhood culinary memories have now happily merged in a marriage that has combined our families' folk-baking traditions.

Within Walking Distance

Because a horse or a child could walk only so far, our rural landscape had been dotted with cheese factories, grade schools, and churches.

When I was a kid, the cheese factory across the road from Otto Fry's house was still standing but had been repurposed as a shed for young cattle. Although the one next to Fry's farm had gone out of business, factories at Rockbridge and Loyd, both relatively short drives from our farm, were still operating, as were others farther afield.

During my boyhood, the milk truck would make daily morning rounds to pick up cans of milk and haul them to the cheese factories, but earlier generations were responsible for transporting the milk themselves. This chore required hitching Dick and Ned to the wagon and hauling the cans from the previous night's milking (cooled in a tank of well water) along with the morning milk to the factory where it would soon become cheese.

When my uncle was in his nineties, he recalled that farmers would not only drop off their milk but also dip into the vats of whey, a by-product of cheese making, to haul home as food for their pigs. My late mother used to tell the story of her father stopping on his way back from the factory to pick wild roses for his young wife.

For those who were not traveling with literal horsepower,

stiles had been constructed for taking shortcuts across neighbors' property. Stiles were a quaint phenomenon, looking much like permanent wooden stepladders but with steps on both sides. Fences could be scaled without the construction of stiles, but if someone climbed a woven wire fence, stepping between the wires, the fence would soon sag. And if someone crawled between tautly stretched barbed wires, clothing, or worse yet, skin, might be snagged.

A couple of stiles remained on our land when I was young, one in our night pasture for crossing the fence that served as a boundary between our farm and that of Frank Brewer. Rather than following the road to the upper Buck Creek School, my father and uncle could shortcut down the valley, cross the stile, and make the trek to school in less time.

Another stile crossed the line fence in our pig lot that marked the border between our farm and Everett Gray's for shortcutting to the Pleasant Ridge School, the one I attended as a boy. But by the time I was a teenager, the stiles had decayed, disappearing into the past.

My mother often told the story of cutting through a woods with her brother on their way to school as first graders. One overcast day in the woods, they heard someone calling to them, "Who? Who?" My Uncle Maynard, who was the older of the two, dutifully answered, "It's only Maynard and Esther Buckta," not realizing that he was providing that information to an owl.

For some reason, Evangelical United Brethren churches proliferated in our area, the nearest one visible from our kitchen window. But another was located down the road at Buck Creek, the same clergyman doing double duty for both churches. Ironically, they were not far apart and each had a tiny congregation, but communities were reluctant to relinquish either their one-room schools or their little churches.

When I was a member of the Pleasant Ridge Youth Fellowship,

we would travel to revival-type assemblies of young people hosted by different EUB churches. In retrospect, I wonder what missionary activity initiated the founding of those churches, all only a stone's throw from one another, within a comfortable walking distance both for children and for horses.

Soon after I graduated from high school, the EUBs were swallowed up in an ecclesiastic merger with the Methodists, and their list of forbidden social sins was somewhat abridged under that umbrella.

Both the church and the school are closed, and fewer farm homes dot the ridge, the distances between them far greater. Nowadays, people drive for transportation and then walk for the sole purpose of using their legs. I remember when farmers would laugh at the idea of walking for exercise.

A few years ago, a physician who lives in a house on upper Buck Creek asked if I minded that he sometimes hiked across the land I own. Of course I told him he was welcome to walk through my woods.

His request made me think of the walking trails that crisscross the English countryside, traditional paths that I have walked, and sometimes run, during my visits. On trips through rural Ireland, I have noticed people walking along roads on errands, carrying cloth shopping bags.

While mega-farm operations have replaced many of the small family farms of my youth, more small organic farms, community-supported agriculture operations, little goat milk cheese factories, and other micro-agricultural businesses have been appearing on the Wisconsin landscape.

Maybe the day will return when life on the ridge will once again be within walking distance.

The Good Life

"He doesn't know what a briefcase is!" one of my city cousins laughed, feigning incredulity at my ignorance.

I was irritated, of course, because I didn't know what an attaché was either. But I knew the difference between a cow and a bull, or a woven wire and an electric fence, or poison ivy and milkweed, unlike my city cousins who were babes in the woods, quite literally.

"That's a bull," I'd say, pointing to one of our cows who had a residual aluminum weening ring, minus the barbs, still in her nose. My city cousins would flee in terror, not knowing the difference between a cow's udder and a bull's scrotum.

Every fence was potentially electric in their eyes. After having been tricked into touching one that was electric, they wouldn't touch any fence, even if it was made of chicken wire. They never seemed to understand the function of a porcelain insulator. And because their mothers had cautioned them about the dangers of poison ivy, they tried to avoid brushing against anything green.

The city cousins were good for laughs. I enjoyed horrifying them by stepping barefoot into a fresh warm cow pie, telling them how good it felt oozing between my toes. In my defense, it was nothing more than chewed grass mixed with digestive juices. And truth be told, it did feel good on summer feet that seldom saw shoes unless we were going into town.

My city cousins, on the other hand, were forbidden to go bare-foot by their mothers, because who knew what terrible diseases they might contract, and certainly they faced the danger of stepping on rusty nails or shards of broken glass, not to mention the fearful menace of snake bite.

One time, I challenged an older city cousin to a foot race on the gravel drive across the road between the barn and the house. He was shod, and I was barefoot. You can guess who won.

My mother's city siblings and their families enjoyed visiting the farm during the summer, sometimes for a week-long stay. The cousins liked playing in the fresh air and open country, and the vacation was affordable for aunts and uncles because food was free for the harvesting on a farm, and beds could be shared. If the visiting adults decided to enjoy a side trip without their children, they knew their kids would be no trouble, as they were always playing outside.

~

Now I laugh as I remember these battles between city and country mice, but the adventures of the city farmers in the 1950s who struggled to make a living by milking cows and working the land are less amusing. Those workers who had tired of the rat race in the city, of traffic and of unreasonable bosses, were eager to embrace the good life. How smart did you have to be to run a farm? they might have wondered. You'd have fresh air, wholesome food, healthy exercise—all free for the taking, practically.

I remember one family who moved onto the farm east of us. Eddie had left a job as a mechanic in Chicago for the new job of farming. While his agricultural skills were seriously limited, he used his mechanical skills to combine the parts of an old corn-binder and silo-filler to successfully create a hybrid corn chopper.

His wife was still a city woman, even though she lived in a farmhouse. If someone knocked on her door, she wouldn't answer it until she had fixed her hair and applied her makeup, maintaining those standards she had refused to leave behind. She had a tighter budget in the country for maintaining her household, but she was resourceful. As her husband was a heavy drinker of hard liquor (local farmers preferred beer), she saved the more decorative bottles and filled them with colored water, lovely accents in her living room.

Their young daughter Faith went to our one-room school wearing frilly dresses, hair ribbons, and sausage curls, unlike the other little girls who were attired like the boys, appropriately for rigorous outdoor recesses.

Her reluctant mother was pressed into service helping with farmwork. Sometimes we'd hear Eddie's voice shrieking across the ridge, "Easy, Alice, easy!" as she attempted to back up a tractor while he held an implement tongue in place ready to be hooked to it.

Eddie didn't know that a farmer avoided driving across a field once it had been established, as the wheel tracks would remain visible for the entire season.

And he complained about the outrageous fees charged by country vets. He did his own cow doctoring, he boasted.

After his two-year adventure in farming, Eddie returned to Chicago. Then we realized the limitation of his veterinarian skills, finding the ravine of his woods littered with the skeletons of his deceased dairy animals that he had left for an open-air burial. He either didn't know about or couldn't afford the "rendering works," as other farmers did when a cow died.

(One of my country cousins tells the story of bringing her city boyfriend home to meet her parents only to have him see a dead cow left in the driveway, a check clothes-pinned to its ear, awaiting the arrival of the truck.)

Another city farmer tried his agrarian skills on a farm down the road from my uncle's place. Ray, too, was from Chicago and had come to the country in part because his young son was already showing signs of being out of control. The boy was in my

grade at our one-room school, and while all of the other boys
knew basic birds-and-bees information from watching animals
on the farm, he filled us in on details, sometimes adding his own
imaginative touches.

Like Eddie, Ray was a heavy drinker filled with bravado, a
neo-agrarian more interested in hiding his shortcomings than
asking seasoned farmers for advice. His farming career came to an
end one morning while he was screaming at his son for taking too
much time fetching the cows. In the midst of his rage, he dropped
dead from a heart attack.

His widow returned to Chicago with her two children. Later,
we learned that the son died during a fistfight at a reformatory.

⌒

During the 1970s, Richland County experienced an influx of city
dwellers looking for the good life in the country. Empty houses,
abandoned when farmers retired or expired and their farmland
was taken over by neighbors, beckoned to them. Some of the new
residents were older established transplants looking for a summer
place, as was one of my city uncles, hoping to live close to nature
and recapture his boyhood.

Others were younger, part of a neo-hippy movement, young
couples fleeing urban congestion for a back-to-basics country
life. One of them published the *Ocooch Mountain News*, writing
of their challenges and successes as they attempted to live off the
land with big gardens and a few animals and to master the skills
necessary for sustainable agriculture and food preservation.

These later transplants seemed to experience fewer of the dra-
matic tragedies of the two city farmers who settled on the ridge
in the 1950s. Some were even successful and ultimately became
organic gardeners or developed dairy goat herds. However, many
returned to the city after the novelty of their experiment in country living had lost its charm.

Steve Bryant, the Storyteller

Other parts of the country might have had a Paul Bunyan or Pecos Bill, but on Pleasant Ridge, we had Steve Bryant. He was the sort of guy that my Uncle Virg would say was "fuller a shit than a baby robin." In short, he was a storyteller, and though he had gone to meet his maker long before I was born, his tales lived on.

My father had pointed out to me the spot where Steve and his family once lived, off double D near where a road descended from the ridge down the Dicks Hill to the south branch of Buck Creek. The buildings had been removed, only a handpump remaining in a field of hay.

I have an old photograph of Steve and his family standing in front of their modest cabin, a row of three or four upturned milk cans behind them. Steve looks scrawny with a short, shaggy beard; a battered brimmed hat; baggy bib overalls hanging from his thin shoulders; thick scuffed boots; and on his face, the wary look of a wild animal being offered a handful of shelled corn.

His wife Hattie is short, a block of a woman nearly as wide as she was tall, a faded flour-sack dress she had no doubt made herself, the hem nearly to the ground, her wispy white hair caught up in but escaping from an untidy top knot, her eyes squinting into the sun, a suspicious look of curiosity on her face, too.

And to the far right in the picture is their daughter, Kitty Mae, the height of her father and the width of her mother, her flour-sack dress a different print but the same design as Hattie's. Her brown hair had been bobbed in the fashion of the time but obviously cut at home. Her smile is self-assured, her posture confident, a woman who knows she can take care of herself.

Kitty Mae shared a short-lived marriage to my great-uncle Cal. He told her during their courtship that he wouldn't drink milk, apparently suffering from lactose intolerance, though he probably didn't know the clinical classification of his disorder at the time. After they were married, so the family story goes, she fixed a hot dish for his supper. When he had finished eating, polishing off a substantial portion of the casserole, she asked him how he liked it.

"Pretty good," he said, patting his stomach. "Pretty good!"

"Ha!" she retorted. "It had milk in it! Lots of milk!"

Cal reportedly threw her out on the spot, and she returned to her parents, where she lived semi-happily ever after. Her ex-husband Cal fared less well. While working on a logging crew in northern Wisconsin, a tree fell on him, according to a far-less-amusing family story. He thought he was okay when he was freed from it, but his stomach bothered him. Not realizing that he apparently had some internal bleeding, according to family tradition, he took a handful of aspirin tablets for the pain and subsequently bled to death.

Cal is buried in the Pleasant Ridge Cemetery, beside the Pleasant Ridge Evangelical United Brethren Church, a nineteenth-century white-frame building with a steeple pointed up toward God. Steve, who is buried in the same graveyard, told people that when he was a young man and the church was being built, he and other men in the neighborhood scalloped wooden shingles with their jackknives to give the steeple a more decorative look. After the church was finished, he said, but before the lightning rod was installed at the apex of the steeple, he climbed up, and using the little square of flatness at the top, stood on his head to impress the men working below. No doubt he looked like a rustic inverted version of one of those stone statues that decorate the spires of European medieval cathedrals.

But as no one took a picture at the time, ridge folk had to take Steve at his word.

Steve, like his neighbors, farmed with a team of horses. Once, he was driving them along a fence row when suddenly a rattlesnake struck. Luckily, he was quick as a cat and dodged the fangs, the snake biting the end of the wagon tongue rather than his foot. No damage was done other than that the wooden tongue reportedly swelled up so much that when Steve got back to the barn, he couldn't get the neck yoke off until the swelling had gone down.

Another time, Steve was driving that same team of horses and a wagon to Richland Center to buy groceries and supplies, an all-day journey as it was a ten-mile trip. On the way home, coming up the Dicks Hill from the south branch of Buck Creek, a cloudburst drenched him as well as the leather traces on the harness. The wet harness stretched so that as the horses labored up the hill, the wagon, with Steve sitting on it, remained at the bottom. When the sun came out to dry the leather traces, they shrank to their regular size, and the wagon jingled up the road, with Steve at the reins, catching up to the horses as they reached the top.

During the process, a bit of kerosene slopped out of a can with a loose cap and sprinkled on the hay that he had brought to feed the horses before their return trip. As Steve figured that most of the kerosene had probably evaporated by the time he had unhitched his team, rather than waste the hay, he forked it into their manger, where they ate it.

But it made them a little gassy, Steve found out the hard way. When he lit his pipe as he walked into the barn the next morning, the explosion blew him out the door. Luckily, no harm was done otherwise.

Steve fared less well when working on a threshing crew, and the belt on the power-take-off broke, slapping him in the groin so hard he ended up in the hospital. When Hattie visited him, Steve raised his gown to show her his bruised black-and-blue nether quarters. "Tee-hee!" she giggled. "Wouldn't it be nice if the soreness went away and the swelling stayed?"

Steve told a number of stories at his wife's expense. One day, when she was walking along the sidewalk in town, an acquaintance pointed out to her that she had broken the heel from one of her shoes. "Tee-hee!" she laughed. "I thought there was holes in the sidewalk!"

One time she made Steve a cherry pie, and at his first bite, he dubbed it her "flint-rock pie" after nearly breaking a tooth. She confessed that she had forgotten to pit the cherries. Another time, she made mincemeat pie, using leftover roast beef that she shredded with a fork; her "cat-turd pie," he christened the confection.

Not necessarily from her cooking, but for a personal challenge, Steve one time decided to see how many days he could wait before he had a bowel movement. He became more and more uncomfortable as the days accumulated, and finally, he had no choice but to answer that call of nature, the resultant stool of such a hardness and length that he was reluctant to part with it. Rather than letting it languish in the pit of his outhouse, he used it to replace one of the sixteen and one-half foot rails in his fence.

Steve's stories were like the ice that formed one very cold day at the Quackenbush place when he was helping thaw the pump, that is, generally defying the laws of nature. As Steve poured boiling water from a teakettle down the shaft, the air temperature was so low that ice formed as quickly as the water hit the iron. So fast, Steve claimed, "It was still warm when it froze!"

Victor, the Pig-Cutter

"What I couldn't do if I had something like that!" Victor laughed, holding up two pig testicles by the cords. He tossed them to waiting sows, who grunted and squealed and jostled each other for the treats. The two successful recipients separated themselves from the others and chomped down their delicacies.

Victor was our neighborhood pig-cutter, one who had learned his craft through a folk tradition rather than attending veterinarian school. His father had been a pig-cutter, too, and probably his grandfather, maybe a long line extending back to an ancestor who met the pigs disembarking from Noah's Ark. After all that time at sea, I am relatively certain that more than two pigs got off the boat.

Each pig-cutter had his own technique, depending upon the school of thought from which he had descended. Some made a horizontal slash across the pig's scrotum while others made two vertical gashes. Victor was of this latter tradition, and like his father, used turpentine as a disinfectant, a choice that in retrospect does not seem medically sound. Rather than severing the cord attached to a testicle, Vic yanked until it detached itself from the about-to-be barrow's body.

His patients squealed their alarm during the procedure and walked even more stiff-leggedly during their recuperation period.

But despite the barbarism of Vic's technique, we never lost a pig to post-op trauma or infection.

Farmers were surprisingly coy in language when they referred to the castration of swine. While the word *castration* was certainly in their vocabularies, I never once heard it used, even when I was a teenager and was regarded as old enough to hear language rated mature. Victor "cut" pigs. My grandfather referred to the procedure as "making little girl pigs out of little boy pigs," a euphemism in many ways more disturbing that a blunt reference to the nature of the surgery. Sometimes male pigs were "trimmed," "fixed," or "docked." The story was once told of an elderly woman who took her dog to a country vet to be "docked," and the old guy, assuming a euphemism, castrated her purebred canine, when in reality she had wanted his tail to be shortened.

Maybe the use of castration euphemisms was in deference to the delicacy of women and children, but I doubt it. Life on a farm was filled with breeding, birthing, and butchering, all spectator events. Rural parents assumed that their children would learn about the birds and the bees firsthand, rendering unnecessary those uncomfortable discussions concerning human reproduction.

One of Vic's three daughters was named Victoria. I suspect that Vic had resigned himself to not having a son, and so his little girl became his namesake. I liked Vicki. Her father had rough edges in grooming, dress, and personality; no one would have been surprised to learn that pig-cutting was his sideline. But Vicki was delicate and finely featured, with pretty hair and a sweet smile. As a little boy, I felt that she was out of my league, even if her dad was a pig-cutter.

I confessed my attraction to her in the hearing of an older boy who encouraged me to press my suit, assuring me that she liked me, too, and it was my responsibility to initiate the relationship.

Nervously, I took pencil in hand and, on a sheet of paper I had ripped out of my Roy Rogers tablet, pledged my troth to her.

She wrote back: "You sure wrote a mushy letter, but I have gotten mushier. I do not like you and do not write to me again!"

Afterward, I learned that I had been set up; the older boy had known I'd be rejected and thought my embarrassment would be hilarious. Because my announced affection for Vicki was more theoretical than deep-seated, I quickly recovered. Still, I felt wounded, and I remembered the gobbling sows while Vic the Pig-Cutter was completing his work.

~

After I had left home for college, my younger brother did the evening milking for Vic on occasions when he and his family traveled to Lone Rock and wouldn't be getting home until late. As was often the case in such arrangements, Vic bartered for my brother's pay, giving him a runt pig rather than cash. At that time, my father had no community of hogs for the orphan to join. The lone piglet slept in the unfinished basement of our house.

While pigs suffer from a bad reputation, in reality they are neither dirty nor stupid. Arnold (as my family called him, after the pig in TV's *Green Acres*) housebroke himself, waiting until morning when someone opened the door outside to answer his call of nature. Perhaps because he lacked porcine role models, Arnold seemed to think he was a dog. When my father and brother went out to the barn for the morning milking, he tagged along with them like a hound and hung out in a manger on a bed of hay as they worked. After the evening milking, he followed them back to the house and bedded down for the night on a pile of old gunnysacks not far from the furnace for warmth.

Every time my father spread manure on fields or took the empty spreader down in the valley to work up wood, the pig loped along beside the tractor like a dog, happy for the adventure and the exercise.

Arnold grew to a size that stressed both the basement steps and my mother's sense of propriety; a dog in the basement was one thing, but a full-grown hog was another. It was a sad day for my father and brother when Arnold the Pig was taken to the auction barn, but with his manhood intact.

∼

One day Vic was squirrel hunting on his land, years after his pig-cutting career had come to an end and with no son to carry on the tradition. One of the local landmarks, Tunnel Rock, was located down the valley in his pasture. The Driftless sandstone outcropping looked something like the prow of an ocean liner emerging from the ridge but took its name from a crevice that pierced the ship from fore to aft, thirty-some feet back from the prow. The tunnel was more of an open crack, but people had called it a tunnel for as long as anyone could remember.

Vic, who was hunting from the "deck" of the ship, shot a squirrel high up in a birch tree. Unfortunately, the dead squirrel lodged itself in a forked branch, and Vic was forced to climb the tree to retrieve his game. A branch broke, and Vic the Pig-Cutter fell many feet to the ground below, tumbling down the hill until he came to rest against a tree, no doubt feeling even more pain than had his long list of male porcine victims. Unable to get up, much less walk, he had no choice but to wait until someone finally came looking for him.

Perhaps some patron saint of the pigs (we're thinking *Lord of the Flies* here) was seeking retribution against Vic for his crimes against hogkind.

The Pressure Cooker

"Oh, he'll cook up in my pressure cooker!"

That's what Julie would say whenever one of her customers at the Buck Creek Station pointed out that the rooster who seemed to rule the roost there wasn't getting any younger. And her comment became a conversational catchphrase for ridge folk: "He'll cook up in my pressure cooker!"

Julie, along with her husband Old Ed and her son Young Ed, lived next door to their combination gas station and mom-and-pop grocery store, a faux log-cabin storefront with a cement block garage adjacent to it, a precursor of today's convenience stores. Customers could buy gas for their cars, have their flat tire repaired, order an ice cream cone for the kiddies, or pick up freshly cut cheese and bologna for sandwiches. It was one-stop shopping if your standards were not too elevated, but more on that later.

First, the rooster: Julie had told each of her customers the story of the rooster who spent his evenings in the stockroom of the store, roosting on stacked wooden cases of empty soft drink bottles, and his days wandering the grounds. He was quite the cock of the walk, a majestic Rhode Island Red with long plumy tail feathers and a regal crown of a comb.

Young Ed had done the evening milking for someone who, rather than paying him in cash, presented him with a live rooster for the family's dining pleasure. But the following Thanksgiving,

Julie explained, she and the Eds were invited to dinner by relatives, and again for Christmas, and even Easter. Subsequently, she had had no occasion to roast him. "But he'll cook up in my pressure cooker!" she'd laugh whenever someone would suggest that he was getting to be a tough old bird.

He had a tough-guy personality as well, frightening children and unsettling elderly ladies when he would aggressively approach his intended victim, crouched down, wings extended, and perform a tap dance with his claws on the gravel, as if he were about to mount a hen. Once, when I had ridden to Buck Creek with my mother to pick up some canning flats, Julie happened to be walking from her house to the store carrying a cardboard box. The rooster assumed the posture of his menacing war dance as Julie approached him. Obviously, this was not the first time that he had threatened her, because without breaking her stride, Julie punted him like a football, the rooster somersaulting across the gravel, ass over applecart, as the men on the ridge would say.

I suspect that eventually the rooster died of old age rather than in Julie's pressure cooker, because she seemed fond of the bird, despite his crotchety nature. She had no doubt become familiar with the routine, letting him out of the stockroom in the morning and then seeing him patrol the parking lot like a watchdog. The jolly threats were no doubt a cover for her tender sentiments.

In every other respect, the Buck Creek Station was not a sentimental place. Julie faithfully planted a garden on the other side of the store every spring, across from the root cellar, but the busyness of the business kept her from tending it during the summer. She would direct Young Ed to cut the weeds between the rows with a lawnmower to buy her some time until she got around to hoeing, which unfortunately never happened.

Julie had little time to tend herself either. She pulled frizzy iron-gray hair into a makeshift knot from which a waterfall of hair escaped about her face and shoulders. She would share her skin problem with anyone who would listen: she'd work up a sweat in the store and then hair would get in her eyes, and then she would get eczema from the soap she used, and then she'd forget if it was a pound or a pound and a half of hamburger you wanted her to grind for you.

People said that Julie wore the same dress all week, wrong-side-out on weekdays so she could wear it clean, right-side-out, to church on Sunday. I'm pretty sure this story wasn't true, but we all laughed at the idea. I think we felt about Julie the same way she did about her rooster.

Old Ed was one of those elderly men who dodder about, wearing pants too big for him, a droopy cardigan sweater, and fish-bowl glasses. While Young Ed primarily took care of pumping gas, checking oil, and doing garage work, and Julie sold groceries, taking items down from the shelves behind the counter for you and assembling them in one of the cardboard boxes saved beneath the counter for that purpose, Old Ed helped in smaller ways. He often sat in a rickety kitchen chair in the corner by the ice cream freezer and pop cooler. He'd make you an ice cream cone (as you tried not to look in the scummy water where the ice cream scoop was kept) or help you in your search for the bottle of strawberry pop hiding under the dark surface of the water in the cooler. And if you couldn't find the fan belt, the fly swatter, the wrench hanging amid the clutter of merchandise on the outer walls of the store, he would immediately point to it from his chair.

Sometimes, if Old Ed and Julie were in the house eating lunch, if Julie was fixing supper, or if Old Ed was lying down for a nap, Young Ed, unshaven and unwashed, would wait on customers in the store, wiping his oily hands on the legs of his coveralls before carefully cutting your hunk of cheese or chunk of big baloney, being extra careful not to actually touch it with his fingers. My mother would never buy any groceries at the store that weren't canned or packaged, and she had learned to be wary of cereals, as one of her neighbors had found little worms in a box of outdated oatmeal.

We felt sorry for Young Ed, who seemed doomed to live the life of a perpetual bachelor due to his circumstances. He was grubby from the moment he began work early in the morning until the store closed late in the evening, and his obligations to the family business seemed to leave him with little time for a social life.

But time heals all wounds, the ridge folk liked to say, and the ticking of the clock eventually rescued Young Ed. When Highway 80 was widened at Buck Creek, the house, business, and tumble-down outbuildings were all purchased by the State Highway Department for demolition. Now the only visible evidence of the former Buck Creek Station is the door to a root cellar carved into a bluff where the Pine River crosses the road. Julie and Old Ed moved into the Pine Valley Manor retirement facility, and Young Ed, although the "young" at this point was a matter of relativity, became free as the breeze once he had received his part of the sale profit. People joked that they didn't recognize him in clean clothes, with a smooth-shaven face and unstained hands. At the funeral of an old Army buddy, he met the widow whom, after a nontraditional courtship, he married. Both were past the years when they might have produced an even younger Ed, but they traveled and eventually bought a house in the South.

Like the rooster that Young Ed had received as payment for milking cows for a friend, he, too, escaped the pressure cooker, the business and the family that he had devoted himself to for much of his life.

Silas Breese

Si Breese was an old man and a widower from the time that I remember him, his wife, Nora, having passed away before I was born. His house at the end of the lane was gray and rundown, most of the paint long flaked off, the trim rotting, the roof leaking.

A woodpile leaned against his house, fuel for an old wood-burning cookstove. In winter, he kept a fire going in it, a coffeepot on a back burner, and then sat with his feet up on the edge of the opened oven door.

Silas had quit farming by the time that I knew him, no longer milking cows, only renting out his cropland. While he didn't keep livestock, he had a dog, one that had gained a reputation on the lane for fierceness. My father told of a time when he had driven his tractor and corn-picker over to Si's to harvest the old man's crop, but the dog snarled and menaced him when he tried to dismount the tractor and open the gate.

Finally, Paw picked up the biggest crescent wrench he had in his toolbox and snarled back at the dog, "You just try and bite me, you mangy sonofabitch!" He opened the gate, drove through, and closed it, the dog warily growling from a safe distance.

The aging Silas had some fight left in him, as well. The Rural Free Delivery mailman (they were all men in those days) deposited mail in a row of boxes set on posts at the end of the lane. With the aid of his cane, old Si limped the distance from his house, collected his mail, and then hobbled back.

One day Si was about a quarter mile from the junction of Si Breese Lane and County D when he saw the mailman's automobile approaching in the distance, according to another of my father's stories. As he had a letter that he wanted to go out in that day's mail, "He ran like a deer, whirling his cane over his head like a helicopter!" Paw exclaimed.

Whoever was listening to the tale was expected to ask, "Did he make it?"

And Paw's reply was, "You bet your ass he did. And then he limped home leaning on his cane."

Not until I was an adult did I hear the story of young Silas's family migration to Pleasant Ridge.* His father, Balemas Breese, was planning to move his wife and children from Indiana to the Wisconsin farm he had purchased, a homestead located at the end of the lane. But an epidemic broke out before he could leave, and as he lay in bed dying, neighboring farmers dug his grave. After he was buried, his wife, Hannah, loaded a wagon, settled her children, including the boy Silas, atop it, hitched up the team, and leaving in the night made the several-days-long drive to Pleasant Ridge in Wisconsin for a fresh start with her young family.

Si Breese remained on his mother's farm until he was the only one left. And now he, too, is gone, and while his father rests somewhere in Indiana, Silas sleeps in the Pleasant Ridge Cemetery.

~

The lane took its name at that time from Si Breese, whose eighty-acre farm marked its end, the last of a string of similarly sized

---

*Census records do not support all the details of Si's accounting of his mother's heroic and life-affirming journey from Indiana to Pleasant Ridge. Nonetheless, Si's tale became a part of the mythology of the ridge and deserves to be told. And maybe it is mostly true!

homesteads that began with those of Charlie Mick and Chauncey Quackenbush near the start of the lane and continued with that of Banjo Schaefer. A hike along the lane was like taking a walk back in time, as each homestead featured a small barn that sheltered no more than a dozen cows once milked by hand and a modest farmhouse with a big garden. Horses had tilled no more than half of Si Breese's eighty acres, the steep remainder of this Driftless topography serving as pasture and woodlot.

Two townships straddle Si Breese Lane: Willow to the east and Rockbridge to the west. The original eighty-acre home place settled by my great-grandfather Isaac Johnson is in Willow, and the hundred-acre addition purchased by my grandfather Charlie Jones, in Rockbridge.

The barns and two of the houses along the lane are gone now, the other houses serving as summer homes for seasonal residents who come to the ridge for a solitary respite from the city, a taste of the good life. Three new houses have lately been built there. And now I own ninety of the hundred acres originally purchased by my grandfather—actually ninety-two, two of them a gift from the county, land abandoned along the Mick Hill when County D was moved to the south side of the ravine. No land could remain an orphan, I was told by county officials; taxes must be collected in Richland County as well as in Bethlehem.

The little house on the one hundred is gone, moved up to the home place and ineptly remodeled when the original Johnson homestead was razed. The indentations in the ground for the foundations of both houses are still visible. And down in the valley along County D, traces remain of the original homestead, that of a man who, according to legend, traded his rifle for land.

And now I have become an old-man day-tripper to Pleasant Ridge, walking along the access road through my cropland to look for morels and check on my renter's fields, or walking the old logging trail in the woods to look at the growth of my hardwoods, or walking to the crest of the bluff with its fabled rattlesnake dens to admire the view down the valley, a setting my son maintains is as beautiful as a state park.

At times, I've considered building a simple house on the ninety-two acres, but even a small house needs a hard-surface drive, a septic field, a well, and electric utility lines. And when I broach the subject of a house on the ridge to my wife, she gets that look on her face that wives during the nineteenth century must have gotten when their husbands announced that they were going to be taking a wagon train west and homesteading land.

Thomas Wolfe wrote, "You can't go home again." I'll probably take his advice.

Cursing Like a Farmwife

When I wish to express contempt for something, I turn to my wife, raise my eyebrows, and mutter the single word, "Sawmill."

"I know, I know," she'll reply, rolling her eyes and quickly cutting me off before I expand upon Granny Jones's crudely dismissive figure of speech. My wife's sensibilities are offended by what she calls bathroom humor. But I grew up on Pleasant Ridge with a family that enjoyed poetic vulgar language, taking no more offense at crudity than I would at a platter of crudités fresh from the garden with a dill and sour cream dipping sauce.

Granny used to say of my other grandmother, a devout churchgoing lady, that she was so pious she wouldn't say shit if she were up to her elbows in it. If you are like Grandma Buckta in that respect, I advise you to read no further.

But if you have a bit of the salty sailor in you, fasten your seatbelt.

If Granny wished to express her disgust at something, she'd grunt dismissively and announce, "I wouldn't have that up my ass if I had room for a sawmill!" and those of us around her would chuckle and nod our heads in agreement.

A more moderate expression of disapproval was her familiar saying, "That's enough to give a dog's ass heartburn!" Anatomically, the figure of speech doesn't hold up well, but we all laughed anyway, as we knew what she meant.

Another of Granny's favorite tropes described something that vibrates or shakes: "shivering like a dog shitting fish hooks," she'd declare.

However, cats also figured into her repertoire of colorful vulgar language. If the road by her house was especially icy and slippery, it was "Slicker'n a greased cat turd."

Hens, too, provided metaphorical service. To express the futility of an endeavor, she'd sniff and declare, "I might as well get a tin bill and go pick shit with the chickens!"

The sound of chickens eating oats out of a tin bucket, she found apt for describing the sound of someone who had hurried into the outhouse during ear corn season to answer an urgent call of nature.

She characterized a disingenuous clergyman as someone whose "prayers rose no higher than the steam off a fresh goose turd." And an effeminate physician of whom she disapproved, in all likelihood "squatted to pee."

Some of her off-color bon mots I may have forgotten, because like her, as I age, "I'd forget my ass if it wasn't fastened on."

While we credited Granny as the author of these colorful figures of speech, I suspect she was merely the conduit for them, that the Johnsons and Davises and Stockwells who were her ancestors may have passed these phrases down through the generations. Whatever the case, like the oral tradition of folk songs, my father, during moments of emotional frustration and distress, could be heard mumbling about tin bills and sawmills, as could some of my cousins, and I confess, this writer, too.

If Granny Jones were to be judged on her vulgar language alone, people might have dismissed her as a dirty old woman. But ironically, she was highly moral in many respects. She had no time for people who smoked cigarettes or drank alcoholic beverages. She found fault with those who violated their marriage vows or who were sexually promiscuous. She condemned those who lied, cheated, and thieved.

A product of her time, she was also intolerant of those who were not white, were not protestant Christians, or were not heterosexual, attitudes shared by many in our family and neighborhood as well.

While I laugh as I remember hearing Granny sputtering her vulgar figures of speech, I also recognize that she was unwittingly instrumental in nurturing my love of language. She never attended high school, and she spoke a substandard dialect. But she was my favorite grandparent, and maybe, just maybe, I can credit her colorful language for inspiring me to become an English major in college and a writer throughout my adult life.

However, if I had ever told her of this positive influence, she probably would have laughed, patted my hand, and dismissed my praise with some comment about steaming goose droppings or canine rectal heartburn.

The Longs and the Shorts of It

Two longs and three shorts meant that someone on our party line wanted to talk to my mother. If she heard the jangling manual ring of the wooden box telephone when she happened to be hanging the wash on the line or carrying water to her Leghorn hens, she dropped everything and sprinted for the house—faster than a speeding pullet, I once quipped.

Ma was a student in high school long before the advent of competitive interscholastic sports for women, but she would certainly have excelled at the hundred-yard dash. However, rather than a starting pistol shot, she would have required the *er-er-er* ring of a crank-style wall telephone.

Not long ago, my wife and I visited a small-town antique shop with wares that included an old-fashioned wall telephone, much like the ones we had each seen our mothers talking on when we were children. I turned to her and said, "Three longs and two shorts." Lu replied, "One long and three shorts."

Those of us of a certain age may have forgotten the numbers of our first rotary telephones, but we certainly remember the longs and shorts of our wooden wall box phones. That early technology has remained vivid in our memories. The "long" required three turns of the crank; the short, a half turn. Several turns of the crank, followed by a pause, would summon the operator, not voice recognition technology that answers your clear enunciation of the word "Rochester" with a mechanical rendition of "Rumpelstiltskin?" but a real live person who understood English and smoothly connected you with your long-distance party. Corporations back then did not try to conceal the phone numbers of people working at their desks as company secrets, nor did they outsource help-line calls to someone in the Philippines, who would answer in a heavily accented voice.

The party line made a telephone clearly memorable. From six to ten customers shared the line, each with a personal combination of longs and shorts. In some respects, the party line was the precursor of social media, but in this instance, you were "friended" because of proximity to one another. My mother, at her three longs and two shorts, would hear and recognize the rings of everyone else and would know whether or not the call might be interesting before deciding to listen in, picking up the receiver as gently as possible to minimize the self-incriminating click.

One familiar number usually provided the opportunity to eavesdrop on what passed for phone sex on the ridge. Ancient blue-haired widow Belle had an equally geriatric boyfriend, Pearlie, who would call her during the afternoon. They would giggle and whisper to one another like teenagers and make affectionate kissing sounds, all to the delighted disgust of those rubbering—the term for listening in on a party line.

Sometimes the information gained by listening in on a conversation proved faulty, just as in the old childhood game of telephone in which a whispered sentence becomes garbled in the passing, as when Minnie, after listening in on and mishearing a conversation between my mother and her best friend Dorothy, sprayed her raspberry patch with the herbicide 2, 4-D.

Hankie was a developmentally disabled adult who continued to live with his mother. When he became bored, the telephone was a source of amusement. If Ma was chatting on the phone with

Dorothy and heard strange noises on the line, she'd automatically shout, "Hankie! You hang up right now!"

Some rubbered stories that neighbors repeated for laughs were probably apocryphal. The elderly maiden lady Fanny, who lived with her also unmarried sister, supposedly called the county agent to ask, "How long does a rooster have to be penned with the hens before the eggs will hatch?"

The agent, who wanted to double check in a reference book, replied, "Just a minute."

"Thank you, John!" she replied, hanging up.

On another occasion, Fanny supposedly called the doctor because her sister was not feeling well and said, "I'll bring in a sample of her pee."

"You mean urine," the doctor told her.

"Oh, no," she answered. "It'll be Martha's."

The telephone was especially important in the lives of farm-wives who wanted to stay connected with other women, as they led relatively isolated lives. One young wife was obviously very lonely when she first left her family and friends behind to join her husband on his farm on Pleasant Ridge. As phoning her mother was an expensive long-distance call, she kept in touch by sending penny postcards, filling them with tiny writing in order to share as much of her life as possible, and then looking forward to the replies.

But like most farmwives, she adjusted to her new life and soon memorized the long-short telephone combinations that not only unlocked hours of entertainment but also introduced her to the community.

Men folk joked about the penchant of their wives for gabbing and gossiping. My father laughed that my mother and her friend Dorothy talked at the same time on the telephone so that they could say twice as much.

Jokes and gender generalizations aside, sociological studies have shown that men have always tended to talk more in general. While women may have dominated the party line, farmers did their talking leaning against tractors or pickup trucks, at feed mills or general stores, on Saturday nights at taverns, and certainly at public meetings.

Conversations have traveled a long distance since my mother's three longs and two shorts, through rotary dials, push buttons, plug-in car phones, cordless phones the size of bricks, flip-tops, and the now omnipresent smartphones. If Ma had been able to put a tiny telephone in her pocket, whether she was at the clothesline or in the henhouse, picking raspberries or hoeing garden, washing milk machines or dumping kitchen scraps over the fence to the hogs, she could have avoided those hundred-yard dashes and stayed connected while she picked peas or gathered eggs, even if her physical fitness might have suffered as a consequence.

Ain't That Pretty

"Oh, ain't that pretty, Aunt Nory!" we'd yell, hurrying through the evening milking, a chore that needed to be done even on a national holiday. We had to finish and get to town before dark, or we'd miss the first part of the fireworks display on the ballfields in Richland Center's Krouskop Park.

I never knew Nora's niece, who uttered those memorable words of appreciation at viewing her first Independence Day fireworks display. For that matter, I never knew the late Nora either, but I knew Si Breese, her husband, who during my childhood was an old man living at the end of the lane adjacent to our farm.

But my family has always been quick to seize a phrase that was filled with a bit of offbeat humor or that particularly characterized some individual and then hang on to it like a dog with a bone. If a medium conducted a séance as the next Fourth neared and successfully conjured the spirit of my father, after all these years, we'd probably still hear him mutter to himself, "Oh, ain't that pretty, Aunt Nory."

The Fourth of July was the high point of the summers of my childhood. It was not because I was filled with patriotic fervor but rather because I was delighted by the spectacle of the fireworks.

During the days leading up to the big event, Paw would sometimes set off a few illicit firecrackers, technically breaking the law but increasing our excitement.

Sometimes Paw placed an empty tin can over a lighted firecracker. The explosion sent it skyrocketing into the air, our dog yelping in alarm from behind the porch. We kids stood with our hands over our ears in mock dismay as each firecracker went off. And yet, with the paradoxical nature of children, we begged our father to set off still another.

Many people traditionally picnic on the Fourth, but not us. If the sun shone, we made hay; if the weather was too wet for haying, it was, unfortunately, too damp to picnic. So, with the exception of Paw's firecrackers, our celebrating waited until sundown.

On the evening of the fireworks exhibition, I hurried the last cow to be milked into the night pasture and closed the gate behind her. I kept a watchful eye on the progress of the setting sun, fretting that we'd get to town too late. Finally, Paw and I had fed the barn cats, rinsed the milkers, and hefted the milk cans into the water tank.

Quickly, we cleaned up and changed our clothes, grabbed a blanket to sit on, threw sweaters over our arms (the park was on a river and cooled off at night), picked up the brown paper grocery bag of warm popcorn, put the two-quart jar of iced well water in another bag to keep it cold, and drove down the road, we kids bouncing on the back seat with excitement.

The throng of people awaiting us in town was intimidating. Usually, Richland Center was a sleepy little burgh, fiercely temperate and doggedly conservative, but on the evening of the fireworks, it came alive, like a maiden aunt taken unaware by a glass of elderberry wine.

Because of our lateness, we'd usually find a parking space at the far end of the park, and then hike the distance to the baseball diamond where the display was set up. All about us stragglers chattered as they hurried along, not only townspeople, but folks from all over the county. Someone in each group was the designated blanket carrier.

Unlike patrons of big-city fireworks, none of these spectators carried intoxicating beverages. Town law strictly forbade consumption of alcohol in public. And no one brought a Frisbee, as they had not yet been invented.

Soon we found a spot to spread our blanket and settled down to eat popcorn and wait for the spectacle to begin. The sun had slipped over the hills west of town, dew was misting the grass, and from the river came the calls of frogs and other night creatures. Occasionally, from some dark corner of the park, the bang of an illegal firecracker rang through the air.

At last the fireworks began. We kids stretched out on the blanket to have a better view. The Kiwanis Club, which sponsored the event, never purchased a large assortment, so they frugally parceled out their offerings, one at a time, waiting until the oohing and ahhing had completely subsided before sending up another.

We lay in suspense, waiting for each burst to materialize. Would it emit a burp and shoot sparkling cascades of reds, blues, and yellows? Ooh! Ahh! Or would it be the surprise bang of an artillery shell, sending faces burrowing into a blanket, toddlers screaming, and babies crying?

All too soon, the display ended for another year, and we'd trudge back to the car. Around us, automobile engines were starting and headlights flashing. Horns honked as auxiliary sheriff's deputies directed traffic slowly emerging from the park, and we turned north on Highway 80, homeward bound.

By the time we had driven back up the ridge, we kids were sound asleep in the backseat of the car. "We're home. Wake up," my mother called to us.

"Oh, ain't that pretty, Aunt Nory," my father teased us. Drowsily, my father, brother, and I lined up to pee outside by the lilac bush while my mother and sister took turns inside, and then we all stumbled off to bed, content that another Fourth of July had been well observed.

Foods of the Ridge

Many people these days are interested in ethnic and grassroots cooking. As I hale from Pleasant Ridge, the haven of some genuine honest-to-God hill people, my roots are about as grassy as any other fellow's. In general, the women I knew were excellent folk cooks. But a few of them have enjoyed a sort of dubious fame over the years for some of their culinary catastrophes.

You may have read about Hattie Bryant's "cat-turd pie," concocted from leftover chunks of pot roast that she had shredded with a fork, or her "flint-rock pie" made from unpitted cherries.

Or Julie's irascible Rhode Island red rooster, a tough old bird that limped outside the Buck Creek Station like a watchdog but, according to Julie, would fix up just fine in her pressure cooker.

But theirs were not the only food mishaps that live on in infamy.

As a young man, my father worked for cousin Mel as a hired hand. One unusually warm fall afternoon Mel's wife stopped Paw at the edge of the cornfield he was picking and offered him one of her by then locally famous treats: warm and runny pumpkin pie. Paw managed a couple of polite bites in Ella's beaming presence, but the minute she disappeared back inside her kitchen, he decided to dispose of the pie without hurting her feelings. A gaunt coon hound that was locked up in a nearby corncrib looked as if he'd eat anything. The dog trotted eagerly to the discarded piece of pie, sniffed, and after turning around three times, lay back down again. Paw had to climb into the corncrib and scrape the ill-fated pie through the cracks of the floorboards with his shoe.

Another kin, cousin Ruby, once concocted a notorious breakfast surprise. Apparently, she had never been able to make her pancakes nice and thick the way her husband Everett's mother had. After suffering from this unfavorable comparison for a number of years, Ruby decided that she would indeed make him a nice thick pancake, just like her mother-in-law once had.

To her inferior skinny pancake, she kept adding spoon after spoonful of batter until she had built up a substantial pancake nearly three inches thick and might have weighed as many pounds. She wryly presented the not-so-hot hotcake to her spouse, who was not amused. He flung it at her, she ducked, and the breakfast entrée thwacked against the kitchen wall, where it stuck for a few moments before plopping heavily to the floor.

Down in the valley, neighbor Maybelle one day had the task of taking grist into town to be ground. She left instructions with her husband for his noon dinner, but he was busy building a fence and didn't pay particular attention. The casserole he found on the table was cold and not too tasty, but Maybelle wasn't celebrated for her cooking, so he ate it.

Not until Maybelle got back from town did he learn that his lunch was in the refrigerator, and he had gulped down scraps destined for the dog's supper.

In defense of these less than exemplary cooks, the adage that proclaims a man may work from sun to sun, but a woman's work is never done, rang especially true for farmwives. While farmers generally prided themselves in not being able to boil water in a kitchen much less prepare a meal, women not only had the sole responsibility for cooking, cleaning, washing, gardening, and other domestic chores, but they were oftentimes expected to help with milking, shocking oats, driving tractor on a hay wagon, tending chickens, and slopping hogs.

And as penance for disparaging these ridge cooks, I have a confession of my own to make.

My mother's kitchen was inviolate. She did not want my father trying his hand at the range, and especially, she did not want me experimenting with recipes. Once, I took advantage of her absence to make one of my favorite snacks, sugar cookies.

For my boyhood birthdays I had requested angel-food cake with frosting in blue, my favorite color. I decided to branch out from that dessert by making my own blue sugar cookies.

Mixing up the cookies was simple: eggs, sugar, vanilla, flour, and butter. But I didn't want to deplete my mother's butter supply. She kept an empty coffee can on the stove to save bacon drippings for frying potatoes. I thought the substitution would be fine.

My cookies were less than a success. First, the blue food coloring combined with yellow egg yolks in the cookie dough to make not a pretty sky blue but a sickly green color. And even worse, the bacon grease gave the cookies the flavor of leftover fried bacon that had been forgotten in the refrigerator.

But Eve, our dog, thought they were the most delicious treat she had ever tasted. And that's the thing about anyone's cooking, isn't it? It's all a matter of catering to your entire family's taste.

Good Gardens

A couple of years after her husband, Steve, had died and gone to his rest in the Pleasant Ridge EUB Cemetery, a neighbor greeted Hattie Bryant in town by asking her, "Have you found a new husband yet?"

"No," she replied, squinting into the sun, a grin on her face. "But I got a good garden!"

That non sequitur amused folks on the ridge, but it held a certain logic, considering what society expected of women at the time. Common wisdom dictated that a woman needed a good husband to be fulfilled, accepting as true the adage that love and marriage go together like a horse and—you know the rest. And just as a farmer had his fields, his helpmate must have a garden, and a good garden, if she were to be an exemplary wife.

Hattie still had her hat in the ring so to speak; if she had a good garden, a good husband might appear in the not-so-distant future.

My mother's garden was a source of pride for her but also a constant concern. "Oh," she'd fret when she found herself bogged down with housekeeping, laundry, and chickens. "I have to get down there and hoe that weedy garden!"

She did not want to be burdened with a reputation for disreputable gardens, like Julia at the Buck Creek Station who would optimistically plant her seeds but, being too busy to tend the patch, in desperation would finally send her son to mow between the rows.

Ma's gardening year began in early spring when she sent me into the woods with a shovel and a bucket to dig topsoil for her. She'd roast a pan of dirt in the oven to kill the weed seeds and then fill three empty cottage cheese cartons that she had saved. In one, she'd plant tomato seeds; in another, bell peppers; and in a third, cabbages. On a sunny kitchen windowsill, the seeds would soon sprout, the tiny plants as thick as spears of grass in our lawn.

When the seedlings were well established, she'd put them on the back steps for longer and longer periods of time until they became acclimatized. And about that time, she'd begin suggesting to my father that it was time for him to plow, disk, and drag her garden. Like most farmers, my father thought that his fields took priority over my mother's garden. Ma knew she had to repeatedly make the request that he get to her garden before he eventually would.

My mother dispensed with stakes and string lines to mark her rows. Instead, she had my father drive the tractor with the corn planter (fertilizer bins full but seed corn canisters empty) over her garden to fertilize it and mark the rows. And then she set out the seedlings she had started and the seeds she had ordered from the Jung Seed catalog.

Some gardeners had a planting schedule rigidly determined by signs. Gramp wouldn't plant corn until the oak tree buds were the size of a squirrel's ear, and Uncle Vern always planted his potatoes on Good Friday. But after my mother stood outside, sniffed the air, and felt the sun's warmth on her face, she would announce that it was time to plant. And once my father had prepared the soil, she did, beginning with an outside row and working across the plot. If she didn't finish planting that day, she did the next.

Ma's garden was standard fare with no time for exotic vegetables. She grew corn and potatoes, peas and carrots, beets and cucumbers, leaf lettuce and Swiss chard, squash and onions.

According to a story she told, when I was four years old and she was planting while pregnant with my little sister, who would be born in July, she had me place onion sets in the shallow furrow she had made with her hoe. As I worked, I repeated as a mantra "Hairs down, tails up, hairs down, tails up," to remember the proper placement of each bulb.

My father, with his rudimentary carpenter skills, built shelves and bins in the basement, where Ma stored her summer canning of fruits and vegetables, jams, and pickles, later adding her autumn harvest of potatoes, onions, and squash.

While farmers seldom helped their wives garden, I learned that my great-grandfather Isaac was fond of gardening, as was his grandson, my Uncle Vern. I inherited the green thumb as well. While I plant my peas early and my squash late, and other vegetables relative to the expected last frost date, I think of my mother's planting style. Her gardens were certainly as successful as any of mine. Gardens seem to have an elastic nature, like babies, and a tendency not only to survive but to thrive. When pushing the seeds into the earth, a gardener plants not only hope but relative certainty.

As a farm boy, I helped my mother tend her garden. Perhaps I took seriously her weedy garden lament and, with the protective concern that sons have for their mothers, hoed beside her.

My great-grandfather's hand-tinted photo hangs in the stairway of our city house, a crinkly-eyed patriarch with a wispy white Colonel Sanders beard. I think of him when I work in my country house garden, using the vintage hoe that I inherited from my mother-in-law. After a decade in Milwaukee where I tried to surreptitiously grow vegetables in my flower gardens, we moved to Door County where at last I had a garden of a size that would rival those of my mother.

But I quickly learned that the gardening techniques that I had absorbed by watching my mother did not work well in northern

Door County. Rather than deep, heavy clay-based soil, I planted in thin, rocky topsoil. My springs arrived late and cold, and the rains took a July hiatus, not resuming until mid-August. I worked the soil as little as possible when preparing my garden for the season, using a layered lasagna approach, as tilling quickly dried the soil. I had to adopt an incremental planting plan, putting in peas, for example, as soon as the soil could be worked, and not even thinking about corn until the second week of June. I laid soaker-hoses along the planted rows and mulched between them first with a layer of newspapers, then with a layer of straw. Once my garden was put in, I retired my hoe for the season.

When I had finished, my fenced-in garden looked as if I had bedded it for horses. I can imagine my great-grandpa Isaac leaning over my picket fence and exclaiming, "What the hell?!"

But as weeds pull easily in mulch, I seldom fret about my weedy garden. And like my mother, my wife and I can tomatoes and green beans; make pickles, jams, and jellies; and store squash and onions for the winter.

When friends ask, I tell them that I have a good garden. But they know that I have kept the same wife for over fifty years.

Uncle Jake

He got up from the easy chair where he had been watching *I Love Lucy*, walked to the wall phone, picked up the receiver, and dialed zero. My little sister and I turned to watch him rather than the TV, frowning as we worried what he was about to do.

When the operator came on the line, my uncle said, "Stop following me, or I'll kill you." He slammed the receiver back into place, and with a job-well-done look on his face, returned to his chair. He picked up the package of Camels from the small table beside him, shook out a cigarette, placed it between his lips, lit it, and exhaled a confident stream of smoke, returning to the comedy and canned laughter on the black and white television screen.

My sister and I stared at one another, wide eyed in disbelief, and then I glanced at the clock, wondering how long before my parents would come in from milking the cows. About fifteen minutes, I figured, a long time to wait.

Uncle Jake* was living with us temporarily until a solution could be found. My mother had told us that from the time he had been a child, her brother had never been "quite right"—a euphemism used to describe a variety of disabilities and mental health issues that people of her generation would have rather not talked about at all. After their father had died, Grandma had tried

---

*In deference to the sensibilities of the past, I have not used his real name.

to keep the family of seven children together on a small farm on upper Little Willow, the kids helping with milking the two cows and tending a huge garden while she worked in the home of a well-to-do farmer and gratefully accepted the charity of others.

My grandmother had her hands full regardless, but Jake was particularly prone to acting out. He used a straw to inflate frogs like balloons and watched them float down the Little Willow Creek. He smashed some glass canning jar liners that my mother had used as dishes for her dolls. And once when he and a cousin disappeared, the family heard mock war whoops and saw the pair running along the ridgetop, au naturel.

Jake's troubled life had been filled with false starts. He volunteered for the Army in 1942 but was discharged after three months. He worked at various times as a woodsman, a farmer, and a welder. He married and fathered two children but became estranged from that family. He moved from city to city, but his mental health ultimately compromised both his work and his personal relationships.

Jake came to live with us after his girlfriend in Madison called my mother to tell her that Jake was in a bad way. He had lost his job and was not paying his rent, spending what little money he had left on liquor and cigarettes. My parents loaded my little sister and me in the car and drove to Madison to collect Jake and take him home.

Years later, I thought of Jake when I read Robert Frost's poem, "The Death of the Hired Man": "Home is the place where, when you have to go there, they have to take you in."

We had taken Jake in even though he frightened all of us. My sister and I had our rooms upstairs, but during Uncle Jake's visit, he was given my bed while Margaret Ann and I shared the safety of a three-quarter bed in my mother's downstairs sewing room.

When my parents drove Uncle Jake to the VA Hospital in Tomah to visit a psychiatrist, my sister and I sat on chairs in the back of the office, as my folks and Jake hovered beside the doctor's desk. The psychiatrist and Uncle Jake smoked cigarettes and talked, laughing at the jokes they told each other, Jake chatting away with the syrupy demeanor of a door-to-door salesman.

"He's fine," the physician said, stubbing out a cigarette and rising to his feet. "Jake just needs some hot meals and a few nights' sound sleep, and he'll be as good as new, as long as he stays away from the bottle." He grinned and wagged a warning finger at Uncle Jake, who shut his eyes and nodded his head sheepishly.

We returned to our farm on the ridge, no one talking as we drove home, windows cracked to let some of Uncle Jake's smoke escape.

Once we were back on the ridge, Uncle Jake turned on the television and settled into his chair. Ordinarily we kids were not allowed to watch daytime TV, but during our uncle's visit, the set was on from the moment he came downstairs in the morning until he went back upstairs at night. He chain-smoked cigarettes and never left his chair, other than to get another cup of coffee, if the pot wasn't empty, and to go to the bathroom. My parents usually kept some beer at the foot of the basement stairs, but during Jake's visit my father hid it at the bottom of the potato bin.

Uncle Jake never spoke to any of us but came immediately to the table when called for a meal and ate silently the food my mother had prepared while standing at the stove, tears of frustration welling in her eyes. Then he returned to the TV at meal's end.

If he made additional anonymous threatening telephone calls, I hadn't witnessed them. But I could hear my parents talking in their bedroom with the door closed, the sound of the TV muffling their muted angry voices.

And then my mother called her city brother and enlisted his support. He came to the farm right away. I learned through overhearing adult conversations that apparently the only way Uncle Jake would receive the psychiatric help he needed was if he voluntarily committed himself to a mental institution. Even at a young age, I knew that was unlikely.

Around the kitchen table the adults drank coffee and everyone but my mother smoked, the room filling with a tavern-like blue haze. My father and Uncle Jake were quiet for the most part while my mother and her brother tried to convince Jake to sign the paperwork.

At last he relented, and once again, holding our collective breath, we drove Uncle Jake to Tomah. After a long day filled with questions and answers and the completion of seemingly endless forms, he officially became a patient at the US Department of Veterans Affairs, where he remained under that agency's care until his death.

My mother, as the eldest of seven siblings, assumed legal responsibility for Jake, and subsequently felt emotionally responsible as well. Periodically my family would visit my uncle. He sat in a chair, restlessly tapping his toes on the floor, continually holding a lit cigarette, three watches on his wrist (none of them working). As he stared blankly into the distance, we waited while my mother attempted to make small talk with him, but his interest in us sharply declined once we had delivered the gift of cigarettes.

Occasionally she would feel guilty about her brother's isolation at the hospital and send my father to collect him with a day pass to be a part of a holiday meal. He was never a problem on these occasions, as I suspect his medication had been increased for the visit. He sat quietly and smoked until he was asked to the table, and then he sat quietly and ate, as if he were a displaced person who did not speak the language.

Uncle Jake may not have thrived at the institution, but he endured nearly fifty years, living until he was eighty. My mother took charge of the funeral, asking a preacher brother-in-law to deliver the eulogy, and her sister, the preacher's wife, to sing. She dutifully called distant cousins to browbeat them into attending the service and then invited everyone to the Richland Center apartment where she and my father lived after their retirement from the farm on the ridge.

My wife and I arrived the evening before the funeral and accepted my mother's invitation to meet our relatives for supper at the local Country Kitchen, where we filled two large booths, the men in one and the women in the other.

The next forenoon the clergyman stumbled through his message as he did not know Jake well, and even if he had, little could be said to memorialize him. After all these years, Jake was finally put to rest, and so was some of my mother's guilt regarding his condition. The funeral, we all knew, was mostly for the benefit of my mother, who had cared for him like a surrogate parent.

In the years since, Uncle Jake has lived on in stories—some amusing, some unsettling—as well as the continuing concern that genetic mental illness and addiction tendencies could show up elsewhere in the family.

At the same time, we have come to view his disability differently, recognizing it as an illness beyond his control. Now as we watch advertisements on television for bipolar medications, I can see how times have changed. While families still struggle with mental illness, most people understand now that the disorder isn't a character flaw, and that simply trying harder to be normal isn't the answer. Instead of hiding the illness away as a source of personal shame or family disgrace, more people have told their stories, lessening the stigma.

Their experiences have helped me realize that while we felt confusion and frustration and anger and isolation dealing with Uncle Jake, we could have taken consolation in the fact that we were not the only people on Pleasant Ridge who were trying to keep the skeleton of mental illness in our closet.

Raspberry Queen of the Ridge

My mother was the unofficial raspberry queen on the Pleasant Ridge of my boyhood.

She wasn't the only one to grow the berries, but her patches were among the largest and had parented many other fledgling berry gardens on the ridge. Every year, we picked hundreds of quarts from her raspberry dominion.

Ma tended three berry plots. The oldest, which was behind the henhouse, had been set out by Granny Jones in the 1930s. The next oldest ran from the apple tree by the pig lot toward the house, a child of the original patch. The newest and by far the largest, a sibling of the second, stretched along the edge of a field west of the clothesline.

Many folks who thought Ma just had a way with raspberries were not aware of the work that went into their care and the time she had spent studying UW–Extension bulletins on berries.

Every fall, she cut off the canes that had produced that year to allow room for the stalks that would bear fruit the following season. In early spring, Paw hauled a spreader of wet straw from around the stack, which they forked onto the patch. At the same time, they added nitrogen fertilizer. Late spring was the time to remove dead canes and prune the live ones to a height of three and a half feet. It also meant pulling weeds and periodic spraying to prevent bugs and disease.

Finally, about the first part of July, the berries came on. We picked every other day, an all-day task. Ma and I started before breakfast while the air was still cool. On a hot July day, a berry patch could heat up like an oven.

Paw didn't enjoy picking berries and was relieved if he had hay to mow or fences to mend. Likewise, my sister would wash dishes and make beds as an alternative to setting foot in a berry patch. My brother was too little to fill his pail faster than his mouth and subsequently was excused from the task.

Granny Jones helped during the peak of the season, driving up from town with Gramp, who immediately disappeared into the fields lest he be enlisted for picking. Granny plopped on a man's straw hat and waded into the berry bushes with a lard pail. A heavyset, white-haired woman in a print house dress, she worked slowly but tirelessly throughout the day.

Ma and I buckled our belts through the bails of our two-quart lard buckets, a technique that freed both hands for picking.

On the kitchen table, the berry boxes were set on cookie sheets and cake pans. As we dumped our pails, we kept track of how many quarts each of us had picked. I was an earnest teenager, but the only way I could out-pick Ma was to start earlier and work longer.

Berry picking was a slow, tedious process. Occasionally, we talked, but generally we picked silently, each alone with a pail and reveries. But once a bit of unexpected drama occurred in the patch. Ma's best friend Dorothy was busily picking when suddenly her shriek pierced the air. Hidden by berry leaves, an unseen friendly tabby cat had brushed against her bare ankle.

After the picking was completed, Ma and I tidied up and drove to town to fill the raspberry orders she had taken over the telephone. Fifty cents a quart for delivered berries was considered good money in those days, and Ma saved it up to pay for something special—perhaps a day trip to the Wisconsin Dells, including a ride on the duck boats, an enjoyable respite from farm chores.

But the best part of Ma's berry business was the eating. We ate berries on our cereal for breakfast, berries with cream for lunch, and berries on ice cream for supper.

Ma made raspberry pie—two at a time—and raspberry "fruzz," a dessert combining fresh berries, set gelatin, and whipped cream that had been created by Granny Jones years earlier to stretch a slim picking. I had inelegantly named that confection fruzz when I was a little boy. And for the coming winter, Ma made jam and packed away boxes of berries in the freezer for winter pies.

Ma Jones continued to tend berries after I had left home, but on a much smaller scale, only enough for Paw, her grown kids, and our families when we came home. But each time I go out in my back lawn and pick raspberries from my little patch, a descendant from Granny Jones's original canes, I remember those days when my mother was the raspberry queen.

Ma Jones's Raspberry Pie

1 quart fresh raspberries, divided
1 cup sugar
2½ tablespoons cornstarch
1 tablespoon butter
1 baked 9-inch pie pastry
whipped cream

In a saucepan, crush 2 cups of the raspberries. In a bowl, blend the sugar and cornstarch, combine it with the crushed berries, and cook about 6 to 8 minutes over medium heat, stirring frequently until the mixture comes to a gentle boil and thickens. Remove from the heat, stir in the butter, and cool slightly.

If desired, reserve a few berries for a garnish before arranging the remaining berries in the baked pastry shell. Pour the cooled, thickened berry mixture over the berries in the pastry, garnish with the reserved berries, and refrigerate at least two hours. Serve with a dollop of whipped cream on each piece.

On the ridge, a pie was cut in six pieces, and many farmers found that they had room for a second piece; today, many cooks choose to cut eight servings.

Granny Jones's Raspberry Fruzz

1 package (3 ounces) raspberry flavored gelatin
1 cup boiling water
1 cup cold water
¾ cup whipping cream
2 cups fresh raspberries

In a 2½-quart bowl, prepare gelatin according to package directions using both boiling and cold water. Chill the mixture until thickened but not jelled, about 1½ hours.

Whip the cream and set it aside. Whip the gelatin, fold the whipped cream into it, and then gently fold in the berries. Chill at least two hours. Makes about six servings.

A Life of Pie

"Pie!" my mother called into the night, her voice as plaintive as that of a child. "Pie! I want to make pie!"

Her shouts became more insistent, more demanding. She crawled toward the foot of her bed on her gnarled hands and steel knees, twisting her sheets around her. "I want to make pie!"

The nurse who hurried into her room on softly cushioned shoes shushed and patted reassuringly, telling her patient that she was fine, that it was night, that she was in a hospital bed, and that people were looking after her.

My mother's life to that point had been one of pie, and subsequently, so became mine. As a college student, I had considered a degree in math, a life of pi, but I missed my mother's version and found that I didn't enjoy numbers as much as I thought I did. When I moved out of the dorm and into an apartment as an English major, I made pie, certainly nothing to compare with my mother's, but pie nonetheless. I bought refrigerated sticks of pie dough, a can of blueberry pie filling, and an aluminum foil disposable pie pan. Using a wine bottle for a rolling pin, I flattened the pastry, assembled the pie, and baked it, the heavenly aroma masking the squalor of my run-down second-floor off-campus apartment.

Many years later, I learned to make pie from scratch, if not as good as my mother's, at least a respectable facsimile. My mother had built a considerable reputation for her pies.

"I have sisters-in-law who have never made a pie!" she would sniff contemptuously. Whenever one of her brothers joined us for a meal on the farm, they knew pie would be the featured dessert, as it was whenever my mother hosted a holiday meal for my father's extended family. For birthdays, she always made a ceremonial cake, but generally it would be supplemented with two pies.

Those of us who lead lives of pie possess the certain knowledge that cake is intrinsically an inferior dessert. "Let them eat cake!" Marie Antoinette purportedly scoffed at the peasants. Note that she made no mention of pie, which she probably was saving for her own supper.

For a pie is made with a potter's hands and showcases the jewel-like wealth of a summer's fruit. Loving hands cut the pie while it is still warm and set it before you, and everyone smiles.

The secret to Ma's pastry was lard. And none of the pastry scraps went to waste; the trimmings left after the pies were assembled were placed on a cookie sheet, sprinkled with cinnamon and sugar, and baked along with the pies. This pie-dough confection served as a warm appetizer in anticipation of the appearance of the pies for dessert.

Pies generally made seasonal appearances in accordance with the fruit we picked on the farm during the summer and fall (apple, strawberry, raspberry, blackberry, rhubarb, cherry, blueberry, pumpkin); the winter and spring pies were often from grocery-store bananas, lemons, or raisins or from homemade mincemeat.

If my mother took a pie to a pot-luck supper, I could recognize hers by the treatment of the crust. She turned over the pastry like the top of a bedsheet along the rim of the pie pan, and then pressed a uniform series of hash marks with the tines of a dinner fork. Her steam vents cut into the middle of the pastry were a distinctive flourish, something like a horizontal *S*.

When I was a college student, leftover pies were auctioned at the end of a Pleasant Ridge Evangelical United Brethren Lord's

Acre Sale supper. When I entered the bidding, I could not believe my good luck as I bought pie after pie for the bargain price of only a quarter each! On the way home, I boasted of my good luck.

After listening to me for a time, my father quietly told that no one would bid against me because I was a college student.

～

My mother recovered from the health crisis resulting from the cumulative effects of old age that had sent her to the hospital, leaving her confused and disoriented, making her cry out in the night her desperation to make pie. Perhaps that episode had resulted in part from her subliminal realization that her health had deteriorated to the point that her pie-making days might be over. I felt the urge to reassure her that I would continue her pie-making tradition.

After she had reached the age that pie-making was behind her, I would take my mother to a pick-your-own orchard to help me harvest cherries. Together we would sit by the kitchen window pitting the fruit. Under my supervision, she would add three-quarters of a cup of sugar for sweetening and a quarter cup of flour for thickening to the five cups of cherries, and I would mix up the pastry in a food processor.

For a double-crust pie, we mixed two cups of flour, one-third cup of cold lard, four tablespoons cold water, one-quarter teaspoon of salt, and processed the mixture with a steel blade. We'd roll the pastry and assemble the pie. I'd brush the top crust with a little milk, sprinkle it with granulated sugar, and bake it at 375 degrees for about 55 minutes, until the crust was golden. After the pie had cooled, the filling would be firmer and easier to slice, but the taste was best when the pieces were warm and messy.

"We made pie together," my mother would proudly tell her friends afterward. "My son and I made a cherry pie."

This was the essence of a shared life of pie, a legacy passed from one generation to another, with love.

Crazy Quilter

Classic Victorian crazy quilts were elegant constructions of randomly sewn snips of satin, velvet, and silk, all in dark jewel colors, the seams covered with elaborate feathery embroidery stitches of silk floss, along with an occasional embroidered motif if the size of a patch warranted the embellishment.

My mother's neo-Victorian quilts, on the other hand, were pieced from poly-cotton scraps and occasional fragments of pure polyester double-knit, left over from the dresses she made for my sister and herself. She ripped threadbare sheets into twelve-inch squares to use as a base for each block and then, with the abandon of a 1960s pop artist, splashed bright, flashy print pieces of fabric across them, turning under and pinning any cut sides, and then afterward, top-stitching the pieces and removing the pins.

Then she discovered that she could hide her seams by sewing on the reverse side and turning the piece over in readiness for the next fabric "shingle," working until she had completed the block.

After she had the requisite number for the quilt size she had in mind, she'd stitch blocks into rows, and then the rows into the quilt top, and while she watched TV, she'd embroider decorative stitches of cotton floss along the seams. The finished quilt was layered with batting and backing, tied with yarn, the edges hemmed.

My mother's quilts were not as elegant as those of her Victorian foremothers, quilters who lived in huge houses on the better side of a city and, as some wags said, farted through silk. Ma was a farmwife who helped slop hogs and milk cows when she wasn't consumed by her own domestic chores. Her life, like her quilts, was made of coarser stuff, and piecing quilts soothed her soul. And her nerves.

My mother was a woman with a fragile psyche. I have boyhood memories involving my uncle, who sometimes worked with my father and joined us for the noon meal. The two brothers had grown up without sisters and sometimes teased my mother about her cooking, their humor springing from male sensibilities. Sometimes she'd bolt for the bedroom and throw herself on the bed in tears while my father and uncle chewed slowly, looking helplessly and unhappily at one another.

When I was older, my younger sister and my mother would engage in furiously heated discussions, arguing until my mother predictably dissolved into tears, at which point I scolded my sister.

As an observer of my mother's precarious emotional state, I had learned to tread carefully regarding her feelings, avoiding confrontations by resorting to end-runs, generally getting my way.

When 1970s-era physicians began writing Valium prescriptions, my mother got in line for hers. And her doctor told her to keep taking her pills and sewing (for her nerves) and she'd be just fine. And sew she did, making herself and my sister new dresses for special occasions. She was a child of the Depression and appreciated the cost savings of a homemade dress. And the proliferation of leftover scraps of fabric called out to become quilts. Some scraps she shared with her mother, who also was a crazy quilter.

Others she took to Ladies Aid meetings at the Pleasant Ridge Evangelical United Brethren Church. When a farmhouse or barn burned, or a farm family member was taken to the hospital after an accident or with a serious illness, the Ladies Aid Society took action by making a consolation quilt. Sitting in a circle on folding chairs in the church basement, they would piece quilt blocks, gossiping as they basted scraps of fabric in place. At the end of the session, my mother would take the blocks home for top-stitching and assembly, and then bring the quilt to the next meeting, where it would be tacked to a frame and tied with yarn, ready for presentation to the family in need.

When I was drafted, my mother made a crazy quilt for my young wife and me, one that she finished by the time that I had completed basic training and been assigned to Fort Bliss in El Paso, Texas. As soon as I was granted permission to live off base, I rented an apartment and flew back to Wisconsin on leave to collect my wife and load our '67 Chevy with as many of our possessions as it would hold in preparation for our drive to the Southwest. My mother presented me with the quilt, I stuffed it in the car, and off we drove.

That evening at a motel, we took the quilt into our rented room and spread it on the bed, reveling under the comfort. In the excitement of being together again and in the anticipation of getting to El Paso as quickly as possible to set up housekeeping, we inadvertently left the quilt in the motel room, not realizing our forgetfulness until we were a hundred miles down the road.

I phoned the motel, asked about the quilt, and was put on hold while housekeeping checked for it. "Sorry," the desk clerk told me. "Housekeeping didn't find any quilt."

That one lost, I'm thankful for the ones I've managed to keep. In the 1930s, America had experienced a quilting revival. I have two traditional (non-crazy) quilts that my mother made during these years, one in a bow-tie pattern and a second in a squares-around-squares design, all in the funky prints of that era. I also have a wool quilt top pieced by Grandma Buckta with fabric salvaged from old suit jackets and coats. Moths had taken a toll by the time it came into my hands. And Granny Jones had pieced a Grandmother's Flower Garden quilt top from tiny hexagons of fabric. Years later my mother paid an elderly quilter to hand stitch it for Granny. I have that quilt, too.

In recent years, the quilts of Gee's Bend have come into artistic prominence. African American women in this isolated Alabama town have a tradition of quilting, neither for recreation nor for decorative arts, but for necessity, for keeping their children warm in unheated shacks. They use scraps of worn-out clothes, assembled with imaginative improvisational simplicity, an effect reminiscent of some twentieth-century abstract painters.

My mother's crazy quilts were also pieced for solace and economy, an improvisation on endurance. I will always regret the lost quilt that she made for me, but I will never forget the night that I slept under it.

When my mother died in 2006, I spoke at her funeral about the prayer that was sewn into those quilts, one in which she said without words that she wanted to keep us warm, to keep us safe, and to keep her love with us. She lived her life like that as well. In my eulogy, her quilts became a metaphor for the strong, complicated, comforting woman we had lost:

One part was her garden that filled a bin in the basement
with potatoes, a freezer with corn and beans, and shelves with
jars of tomatoes and applesauce and pickles and jams. When
I make a batch of strawberry preserves, when I can tomato
juice, or when I dig potatoes, I hear that prayer.

My mother was queen of the raspberry patch, and once
you could have shared her bounty for fifty cents a quart. She
knew pretty much all there was to know about raspberries,
and when I mulch mine or pick the first ripe fruit of the season, I hear her prayer.

I never liked her chickens, carrying water to the range
house in the summer, or choosing the young rooster that
she sold live for a dollar, a dollar and a quarter dressed.
When I crack an egg or cut up a fryer, I hear a prayer from
my mother.

My mother sewed clothing not only for herself but for all

of us. When I sew on a button or stitch a ripped seam, I hear a prayer from my mother.

She taught generations of first graders to read and helped to open for them the magic of books. She helped me with my reading when I started first grade. I finally caught up, and when I discuss literature and writing with my students, I hear a prayer from my mother.

Because my mother taught before 1937, she had needed only one year of county normal for a lifetime teaching certificate. She finished her bachelor's degree when she was fifty-something after taking night and summer classes while teaching full time. It was a celebration to remember after she and her best friend Dorothy Johnson graduated! When I think of my degrees, they pale in comparison with my mother's, and I hear a prayer from her.

My mother cooked for threshers, for extended family, for anyone who was in need of a meal. We called her for advice: How long do you cook a pot roast? Can I have your recipe for sauerkraut cake? Now when I make yeast rolls, when I bake a pie, when I fix beets and Swiss chard from my garden, I hear a prayer from my mother.

When I held my own children as babies, I heard a prayer from my mother.

At the hospital, my wife told my dying mother that she would always take care of me. Those of us who are fathers and sons can never give the love a mother gives; we can only receive it.

The memory of my mother's life wraps around me like one of her crazy quilts (life can be a little crazy at times!), and now as I step back, her life comes more clearly into focus. That memory keeps me, and everyone who knew and loved her, warm and safe and tucked in with love.

Searching for My Father

After I had become an adult, my father and I took winter walks from the farmhouse on Pleasant Ridge along Si Breese Lane to and from his family's long-abandoned house. While those two-mile hikes occurred at different times of the year, in my memory the season was always winter, the ground snow-covered, the air frosty, the leafless trees dark silhouettes, the evening sky alive with bright stars, and the moon a beacon. The landscape seemed to have taken its inspiration straight from *The Night Before Christmas*:

> The moon on the breast of the new-fallen snow
> Gave a lustre of midday to objects below.

I was a beer drinker in those days, and my father and I typically would do real damage to a twelve-pack before we set out on our trek, usually waiting until ten o'clock or so to depart. My wife and mother would shake their heads and smile indulgently, knowing that we'd be on foot, and should one of us walk into a tree, no serious harm would be done, to the tree nor to ourselves.

When we returned, my mother would have prepared a bedtime lunch, which my father and I would eat while drinking a final beer, and then we'd all retire for "our long winter's nap."

I felt like I finally found my father on such nights.

◦

My father had never abandoned our family, even for a day. He had not run off with another woman, had not been incarcerated for a crime, nor had he lost himself to drugs and alcohol. But of three siblings, I was the only one who felt I had to search for him. An analogy might explain what I mean.

From down the Dicks Hill at the head of the upper Buck Creek valley, we could hear the eerie cries of Eithel's peacocks, exotic birds that roamed the lawn of her family's small dairy farm as if it were a private garden in Hyde Park rather than Rockbridge Township.

Peacocks, of course, were not native to Richland County, but Eithel found a mail-order source for fertilized peacock eggs and enlisted the surrogate service of a setting hen. I can imagine the thoughts of a Rhode Island Red watching as peacock chicks emerged from her nest. "What a night I must have had!" she'd mutter, scratching her forehead with a claw. "I don't remember that rooster at all!"

And how confused that hen might have been as her chick grew up into nothing resembling herself.

As a boy, I lacked the splendor of a peacock, but I was no less exotic in the eyes of my father. Although he was a dairy farmer by default, we all knew he had wanted to be an auto mechanic. My mother laughed that if she had been born with a motor, my father would have loved her even more.

Paw always drove the best automobile he could afford and at various times owned snowmobiles and a motorboat. His favorite spectator sport was stock car racing, and automotive mechanical malfunctions—stories of engine problems and the repairs ultimately made—were a favorite topic of conversation. Such stories often involved one-upmanship of some sort: a lowly garage man cleverer than his supervisor, an amateur mechanic who gave sound advice to a professional, and sometimes, tales of his own troubleshooting triumphs.

I, on the other hand, couldn't have cared less about the inner workings of an engine, and I was a silent sports guy. I did not consider driving a snowmobile, a motorboat, or a motorcycle a sport; I was a runner, a swimmer, a cyclist, a cross-country skier, all sports.

One summer during a visit of city relatives to our farm, my little brother and I were relegated to the three-quarter-sized bed in my mother's sewing room. Ma's brother Virgil and his wife had our bed, the two girl cousins crowded in with my sister, the boy cousin too young for his own bed.

On the occasions my uncle visited us on the farm, beer flowed freely, and while my brother slumbered beside me, I was kept awake by loud voices and laughter in the living room and the smell of cigarette smoke wafting under the sewing room door.

And then suddenly the door opened, casting a beacon of light across the bed, and I froze, feigning sleep. My father and uncle stepped into the room, unsteady on their feet, each clutching a bottle of Blatz. "Ain't he something," my father stage-whispered.

"Jim, Jim," my mother hissed at him from the living room. "Don't wake those boys up!"

My father ignored her, and I closed my eyes even tighter, wishing that I could shut my ears as well, because I knew that I was not the son who was "something."

"He's going to be a real baseball player someday," my father continued. "You should watch him bat gravel in the driveway! Each one would be a home run!"

When I played 4-H softball, I was lucky when I managed to hit a single.

"And he could be a race car driver," my father added. "He doesn't walk, he runs. And when he does, he's always making a motor sound." My father imitated the sound that was my brother's imitation of a motor.

I made three attempts before I finally passed my driver's test, and the instructor cautioned me about driving in a big city.

My mother appeared, a third figure in the doorway, and scolded the two men. "You guys get out of there now and let those boys sleep!"

Those differences translated into farmwork as well. My father lived for farm machinery. He preferred internal combustion horsepower to literal horsepower, having once as a young man lost patience with a horse and punched the animal, breaking his hand in the process. Because of the marginality of the farm, as a young farmer he could afford only used machinery, but fortunately, he had taken a class in welding. My father, it seemed, spent half of his time using the hay-baler or the corn-picker or the chopper, and the other half hooking up his welder to fix it.

I remember my mother and I returning from a trip to Richland Center when we approached the farm and saw a hammer flying across the road, much like a boomerang. Obviously, the repair was not going well.

By contrast, I was happiest working in vegetable or flower gardens and tending animals. Milking cows could at times be tedious, but not compared to endlessly riding a tractor cultivating corn. The cows had names and personalities, and the routine of milking them was relatively contemplative, the thudding of the vacuum pump powering the milking machines like a mantra. I memorized dialogue for roles I had been given in plays and scripts that I was reciting for forensics.

My father and I sometimes made connections through literature, but the contact was tentative, like Michelangelo's God and Adam pointing fingers at one another but not quite touching. While I earned graduate degrees in English, my father had quit school at the end of his eighth grade. Still, as a student, my father had been required to memorize poetry, and although he didn't particularly care for verse, he was good at memorization.

Sometimes when we were milking cows, he recited poems, and from him I learned the openings to Longfellow's "Village Blacksmith" and Whitman's "O Captain! My Captain!"

But the connections were transitory; I feigned interest when he spoke of automotive mechanical failures, as did he when I waxed literary. And most of the time in the barn, we were ships passing in the night as we milked the cows.

But the winter walks along Si Breese Lane were different than when my father and I milked cows or made hay. In the bleak midwinter when we hiked Si Breese Lane, figuratively speaking, our fingers touched.

My father retold stories as we walked by houses no longer occupied, about Si Breese's mother in Indiana harnessing a team of horses and loading her children into a wagon, after her husband died of cholera, and driving them to Pleasant Ridge for a new start.

No buildings remain where John Pugh and his wife once lived on the road leading down into the valley, the roadbed now nearly hidden by the undergrowth of the woods. The grave of John's baby was unmarked.

Banjo Schaeffer cooled his coffee by slopping it over the brim of his cup and then slurping it from a saucer. He was a skinny man who wore bib overalls that were too big for him, unbuttoned at the sides, and once when he was milking cows, one coughed as she pooped, with predictable results.

Don Armstrong and his wife, Tillie, were driving home from a winter afternoon visit to a tavern and found the Mick Hill slippery. She got out to push, he found traction, and in the fog of his libation, forgot her. "Oh," he said much later when she walked in the front door, "I wondered who that old woman was I saw in the rear-view mirror walking up the hill!"

I heard again the stories of Barney Mick and Chauncy Quackenbush and Frank Reed, farmers gone not only from Pleasant

Ridge but from life itself. And when my father and I returned
home, we were invigorated not only from the exercise and the
crisp cold air but from the connections we had made over our
shared stories on the ridge.

I had, for a time, found my father, and I suspect that he might
have found his son.

Burying My Father

Softly, like a child's breath blowing out candles on a cake, a gentle breeze eased across the ridge on the day we buried my farmer father in the Pleasant Ridge Evangelical United Brethren Cemetery. The April sun warmed the graveyard, as if teasing roots of old roses and day lilies, lilacs and bridal wreaths, to send up early blooms. The grass was green on my mother's plot, where she had been buried three years earlier.

People had gathered in the cemetery with smiles on their faces. They exchanged greetings, happy to see one another, any expressions of sympathy already made at the visitation, life now moving on.

At first, I didn't recognize the short elderly man who approached me, hesitated, and then took my hand. I gave him an uncertain smile. "Darold," he said. "Darold Fairbrother."

"Oh, I'm so pleased you came," I said, taking his hand in both of mine. He had been my first-grade teacher at the Pleasant Ridge one-room grade school. The position had been his first after graduating from the county normal, and he was probably no older than nineteen or twenty at the time. Coincidentally, my mother had been his teacher.

When he was mine, he had loomed large in my life, overwhelming me with his enthusiasm and zest for life. And he seemed worldly to farm kids; some of us had spotted a package of cigarettes only partially hidden on the front seat of his car.

One evening, he visited my parents, and as he walked in the door, he called out, "Northern Lights! They're beautiful!" And he gathered me up in his arms with an unexplained urgency and carried me outside in my pajamas to view the otherworldly frozen fireworks in the northern sky.

In the cemetery he seemed small and old, as if he had been shriveled by time.

But I immediately recognized my cousin Brian, a onetime city boy who had since moved to the country and taken up rural ways. He wore new bib overalls to the funeral, as if he were one of those men patiently smoking in a corner of the cemetery, waiting for the interment to conclude so they could refill the grave, collect their checks, and go home to their waiting families.

When my wife and I had married, he was a precocious little boy who could recite nursery rhymes. Now he lived in a vintage mobile home with his waitress wife and their children, hoping to make his fortune as an inventor. He shook my hand, bear-hugged my wife, and with misty eyes exclaimed, "Gosh darn, I really liked Uncle Jim!"

And the Motts, my old Youth Fellowship advisers at the Pleasant Ridge EUB Church, were there, too. They had been a young pair with a little boy at the time. Now with gray hair and glasses, one patted my hand while the other exclaimed, "We're both so proud of you!"

Their talk took me back to my youth, when as a student in Vacation Bible School I had played tag in the cemetery with the other budding "Christian soldiers." While I was a teenager, the Youth Fellowship had taken on the Herculean task of mowing the cemetery as a fund-raising community-service project.

Beyond the late Vic Crary's fields to the west, I could see the house where I had been raised, and I had the strange sensation that the spirits of my family in their younger years were still gathered in our kitchen, looking out the window at the activity in the church cemetery, wondering if they knew the person who had died and gone to rest in the country graveyard.

The white frame church with its tall belfry and steeple was empty now, but my father's grandparents had been among the early parishioners, and while my family was only casually Christian, we nonetheless had attended Easter and Children's Day services, Christmas programs, Mother-Daughter and Father-Son banquets, and the annual Lord's Acre Sale.

The tolling of the church bell had been a reassuring sound for all of us across the ridge, not only the faithful group gathered to hear Reverend Matthews's homespun sermons.

Paw had gone to church only for special occasions, and then afterward made vulgar jokes about the clergyman conducting the service. But during his older years, he began attending more regularly with my mother and continued the custom after her passing.

When the interment ceremony ended, people lingered in the graveyard, chatting, catching up, visiting graves, and retelling stories from the past. And in one corner of the cemetery, the gravediggers smoked as they waited, and the funeral home personnel hovered near the grave, visibly restless.

Finally, one of the men in dark suits approached me and discreetly whispered in my ear, "Perhaps you could encourage people to move on to the luncheon."

I nodded. Uncle Vern, who lived only three miles away, was serving mourners food at his farm.

As the eldest son, I assumed the role of host, moving about the group thanking them for attending the service and encouraging them to join us for lunch. They smiled and slowly, reluctantly, began drifting toward their parked cars.

I waited until everyone had departed, the empty black hearse driving west toward Richland Center. In the deserted cemetery, the sun beamed brightly, beatifically burnishing the men in work shoes and overalls who shoveled a small field of clay over the late retired farmer, my father.

We were the last mourners to leave, my wife and I, following the others who had gathered to celebrate a long life lived on the ridge.

When my parents were still alive, when my children were restless babies in the back seat, we were coming up the Mick Hill when my young wife commented, "This is a long way from Milwaukee." She wasn't just speaking of the miles that we had traveled from the East Side, but a journey in time as well, back to the Pleasant Ridge of my boyhood.

The death of someone that you love inevitably evokes a sense of loss that extends beyond the person you leave at rest. Driving across the ridge, I passed farms where strangers now live. The landscape had changed, old buildings razed and new ones sprung up like weeds. Many of my schoolmates had departed, and those who survived had become senior citizens like me.

I take consolation from the part of the family farm that remains with me, the company of relatives who still remember, and the artifacts I have collected: the teacher's desk from my grade school, Granny's round oak table, Gramp's mission-style rocker, Ma's good dishes, and Paw's post-hole diggers.

You can take the boy off the farm, but the farm remains, forever.

Acknowledgments

During the 1970s on Milwaukee's East Side, around the time my wife and I had purchased our first house and had begun our family, I began publishing my ridge story recollections in the old *Milwaukee Journal* and *Milwaukee Sentinel*. On returns to the ridge to visit my parents when we were driving up the Mick Hill, my wife would say, "This is a long way from Milwaukee!"

And perhaps that distance, along with the fact that with my children I was expanding a family tree with roots extending back to the American Revolution, brought those tales into a sharper focus.

"You should publish your stories in a book," my wife suggested from time to time. And at last, I have. Without her encouragement and help reading my drafts, perhaps *Ridge Stories* would never have become a reality.

Also helpful in the writing of the book have been family patriarch Uncle Vern Jones, who has always been in my life, and my cousins, the Jones boys and the Johnson kids, who have been enthusiastic supporters of the project.

I thank Press Director Kate Thompson, who offered the encouragement I needed to bring the book to fruition, and especially my editor Erika Wittekind, who has skillfully helped me coax these stories into sitting up on their hind legs and behaving nicely.

About the Author

Gary Jones was raised on the farm purchased by his great-grandfather on a ridge
in Willow Township in Richland County,
where he attended the Pleasant Ridge
grade school and Ithaca High School.
The Joneses could see the Pleasant Ridge
Evangelical United Brethren Church from
their kitchen window.

PHOTO BY BEN JONES

From an early age, Jones knew he
wanted to be both a teacher and a writer. In pursuit of that goal,
he earned a bachelor of science degree from UW–Platteville, a
master's from UW–Madison, and a PhD from UW–Milwaukee,
all in English.

Jones's career in education began in 1966 at age twenty-one at
Weston High School and ended at age seventy at UW–Platteville,
where he taught the same freshman English class he had taken
more than fifty years earlier. His writing avocation began as a
freelance journalist for the Milwaukee newspapers in the 1970s,
while teaching at St. Francis High School. Since then he has written for several Door County newspapers and published poetry,
fiction, and plays.

He met his wife, Lu, during their senior year at UW–Platteville,
and the couple married following graduation, later becoming parents of a daughter and son. Now they spend winters in Platteville,
an easy drive from Pleasant Ridge. Their home in Door County
is now their summer place.